WARRIOR 168

FRENCH MUSKETEER
1622–1775

RENÉ CHARTRAND   ILLUSTRATED BY GRAHAM TURNER

Series editor Marcus Cowper

First published in Great Britain in 2013 by Osprey Publishing,
Midland House, West Way, Botley, Oxford OX2 0PH, UK
43-01 21st Street, Suite 220B, Long Island City, NY 11101, USA
E-mail: info@ospreypublishing.com

A CIP catalogue record for this book is available from the British Library.

ISBN: 978 1 78096 861 2
E-book ISBN: 978 1 78096 862 9
E-pub ISBN: 978 1 78096 863 6

Editorial by Ilios Publishing Ltd, Oxford, UK (www.iliospublishing.com)
Index by Sandra Shotter
Typeset in Myriad Pro and Sabon
Artwork by Graham Turner
Originated by PDQ Media, Bungay, UK
Printed in China through Worldprint Ltd.

13 14 15 16 17 10 9 8 7 6 5 4 3 2 1

www.ospreypublishing.com

ACKNOWLEDGEMENTS

I am grateful to Francis Back in Montreal, Giancarlo Boeri in Rome, the staff
at the Musée de l'Armée in Paris, at the Anne S. K. Brown Military Collection
at the Brown University Library in Providence (USA) and at the Research
Centre of the Canadian War Museum in Ottawa for sharing much
information as well as providing the encouragement to craft this study. All
this material could never have come together in a handsome book without
the fine editorial work and kind coordination of Marcus Cowper at Osprey.
To one and all, I extend my heartfelt expression of deepest gratitude.

AUTHOR'S NOTE

When I was a boy, like so many others for well over a century, inspired by
Alexandre Dumas's novels and the cinema productions based on them, I
played at being a King's Musketeer with a crude wooden sword and a
makeshift cassock; as a historian and curator, I had the wonderful
opportunity to see documents and objects relating to that extraordinary
corps and, as a senior person, I am now writing about them with
fascination. Was the iconic King's Musketeer fiction or was he real?
Certainly this slim volume has much information about the real aspects of
a musketeer: his world, his friends, his enemies, his outlandish bravery, his
life's mission, as well as his distinctive costume and weapons. Yet, there is
more; the musketeer's indescribable aura, intrigues at the very height of
power and mysteries that will never be solved because of oaths of secrecy.
It sounds like fiction, but much of it was real enough and worthy of
boyhood dreams.

ARTIST'S NOTE

LIST OF RANKS

Capitaine	Captain (the king)
Capitaine-Lieutenant	Captain-Lieutenant
Lieutenant	
Sous-Lieutenant	Sub-Lieutenant
Enseigne	Ensign
Cornette	Cornet
Maréchal-des-logis	senior NCO such as a warrant officer
Brigadier	senior NCO such as a sergeant-major
Sous-brigadier	sergeant
Porte-Étendart	Standard-bearer
Porte-Drapeau	Colour-bearer
Fourier	quartermaster-sergeant
Mousquetaire	Musketeer
Tambour	Drummer
Hautbois	Flautist

(Compiled from the 1739 *Cinquièmee Abrégé de la Carte Militaire de France*,
pp. 16–17)

CONTENTS

FRENCH MUSKETEER 1622–1775

INTRODUCTION

On a fine day during the year 1700, a work was published under the title *Mémoires de Mr. d'Artagnan, Capitaine-Lieutenant de la première Compagnie des Mousquetaires du Roi, Concernant quantité de choses particulières et secrètes Qui se sont passées sous le Règne de Louis le Grand* (*Memoirs of Mr d'Artagnan, Captain-Lieutenant of the First Company of the King's Musketeers, concerning a quantity of private and secret events that occurred during the reign of Louis the Great*). Its publisher was Pierre Marteau in Cologne, Germany.

At least, that is what was printed on the title page. In fact, there was no publisher by the name of Pierre Marteau in Cologne or elsewhere. For some 40 years, anonymous publishers of French books had used the name of this non-existent publisher in instances when they would not obtain the approval of the royal censors. Moreover, the books were not even published in Cologne.

The book itself was written by Gatien de Courtiz de Sandras, born in Montargis, France, in 1644 and – this is where it becomes interesting – he had been a King's Musketeer for some 18 years before becoming an officer in the elite Champagne Regiment. His real ambition was to earn his living as an author and, in 1688, he left the army and went to Amsterdam with a number of his manuscripts. These were mainly apocryphal memoirs of French political figures, historic accounts, novels and somewhat political pamphlets, and they seem to have had some literary success. Then, in 1700, his memoirs of d'Artagnan appeared. As a young musketeer, he had surely seen Capitaine-Lieutenant d'Artagnan, who was already something of a legend in his own time, before his death in 1673. So, it is possible that some of Courtiz's memoirs of d'Artagnan contain many true facts (but also others that cannot be verified). The French censors certainly thought so. When Courtiz came back to France in 1702, he was promptly arrested and shut in the Bastille for nine years. He died in Paris during May 1712, shortly after his release. Three years later, Louis XIV, the 'Sun King', passed away, the glow of his reign faded and d'Artagnan was soon totally forgotten.

Nearly a century and a half later, in the early 1840s, the prolific novelist Alexandre Dumas (1802–70) came across Courtiz's apocryphal memoir of d'Artagnan. These memoirs in particular, as well as several other reminiscences from French noblemen of 17th-century France, inspired Dumas to come up with the extraordinary plot contained in *The Three Musketeers*. This novel was first serialized in the Paris newspaper *Le Siècle* from March to July 1844. The story's success was outstanding and it was soon put out in book form. It was translated into English in 1846 and before long it was an international

success. Eager to follow up with another bestseller, Dumas was already busy writing *Twenty Years After*, which was serialized from January to August 1845 before becoming another bestselling book. The public had a passion for the adventures of d'Artagnan and his companions, so Dumas wrote another sequel, *The Vicomte de Bragelonne: Ten Years Later*, also initially serialized in 268 chapters from 1847 to 1850. This included a sub-novel with the title of *The Man in the Iron Mask* that became famous in its own right. The three novels became known as the d'Artagnan Romances.

King Louis XIII, c.1630. In 1622, he founded the King's Musketeers. The two women represent France (at left) and Navarre (at right). Painting by Simon Vouet. Musée du Louvre, Paris. (Author's photo)

Trooper and trumpeter, Cardinal Richelieu's Guard, 1628. The trooper has a red cassock with a white cross. The trumpeter wears the cardinal's red livery and his trumpet banner is embroidered with his coat of arms. Print after Marbot. Canadian War Museum, Ottawa. (Author's photo)

The fictional musketeer Athos was an actual musketeer named Armand de Sillègue d'Athos d'Autevielle. Born in about 1615, he did not have much in common with the fatherly figure in the novel since he was actually quite young. He entered the King's Musketeers around 1641 and was buried in Paris on 22 December 1643, having died from the results of wounds most likely sustained during a duel.

Porthos was simply a fictional character whose name was borrowed from the real-life Isaac de Porthau (1617–1702), born into a military family in Pau, in Béarn. His name appears in two 1642 rolls of the Gardes Françaises Regiment; it is uncertain if he actually served in the King's Musketeers. He soon left the service, possibly because of battle wounds, and was for a time on the garrison staff of the citadel of Navarrenx, which was the sort of position often filled by invalided military men.

The novels' fictional musketeer René d'Aramis de Vannes, or Aramis, was based on Henri d'Aramitz, born in Béarn in about 1620. He entered the

King's Musketeers around 1641. He probably went back to his native province in 1646 and quietly passed away there ten years later.

As for Charles de Batz de Castelmore d'Artagnan, he was also a real musketeer and differs from the above three musketeers in that the events of his life more closely resemble the plots of Dumas's novels and Courtiz's apocryphal memoirs. Several historians have carried out research to find out who the real d'Artagnan was and what his achievements were. We note in particular *D'Artagnan, mousquetaire du roi* by archivist Odile Bordaz. While Dumas gives a real sense of the social and political atmosphere of 17th-century France, he used artistic licence with regard to actual events and timelines. For instance, in *The Three Musketeers*, d'Artagnan arrives in Paris in the mid-1620s and there links up with the three musketeers. In fact, the first trace of d'Artagnan being in the King's Musketeers was in 1633 when, on 10 March, he is listed as an ordinary, and undoubtedly quite young, member of the unit. He was indeed the younger son of a proud but not very wealthy gentleman in the overpopulated and poor province of Gascony in south-western France. Born between 1611 and 1615, he seems to have come to Paris in about 1630. After 1633, there is no documentary evidence of him until 1646 when we find him as 'one of the gentlemen' in the service of Cardinal Mazarin, the prime minister and the most powerful man in the kingdom, at a time when King Louis XIV was just a young boy. Unflinchingly loyal to the royal family, d'Artagnan found himself in the midst of delicate and secret missions during the 'Fronde' revolts and the teenage king would never forget his loyalty. In 1655, he became a captain in the Gardes Françaises Regiment and, in May 1658, was back in the King's Musketeers as its second lieutenant, which was in actual fact a promotion. By 1667, he was captain-lieutenant of the 1st Company, which made him its commandant since the king himself was the captain. The musketeers served in close proximity with the king and, from 1661, Louis XIV entrusted d'Artagnan with carrying out some extremely delicate missions. These were performed successfully, but d'Artagnan was happiest on the battlefield with his men. Reputed to be extremely brave, his end came on 25 June 1673 while charging the fortifications of Maastricht. Louis XIV, deeply affected by the loss, arranged for a funeral mass to be held in his memory in his private chapel and the renowned poet Saint-Blaize wrote a poem, the last lines of which were 'D'Artagnan and glory share the same coffin.'

In his day and ever since, d'Artagnan has been the most famous of the King's Musketeers. Like every young man entering the unit, he had hoped to rise to command and he was outstandingly successful. But what was it like to be a King's Musketeer? Who became one? And what sort of military career would he pursue? For that matter, what kind of unit was the King's Musketeers? What was it that made it special amongst the king of France's guard units and its members so distinctive? This humble work will attempt to lift a corner of the veil on the life and times of a King's Musketeer.

CHRONOLOGY

1610	Assassination of King Henri IV on 14 May. His eight-and-a-half-year-old son becomes King Louis XIII, but Queen Marie de Medici actually governs France as regent until 1622.
1622	King Louis XIII adds a company of musketeers to his guard. They become known as the Mousquetaires du Roi – the King's Musketeers – to serve both on foot and mounted.
1624	Cardinal Richelieu appointed prime minister.
1627–29	Siege of La Rochelle held by Huguenots starts in September 1627 and the city surrenders on 28 October 1628; campaign in Piedmont to contain Spanish with battle at Pas-de-Suze on 6 March 1629.
1634	On 3 October, King Louis XIII appoints himself as captain in chief of his guard's musketeer company. Actual command is exercised by Captain-Lieutenant de Tréville.
1638	Birth of Louis XIV on 5 September 1638; France is at war with Spain and Austria from 1635.
1642	Death of Cardinal Richelieu on 4 December. He is succeeded by Cardinal Mazarin.
1643	Death of King Louis XIII on 14 May. His five-year-old son becomes King Louis XIV, but a regency under the control of Queen Anne of Austria and Cardinal Mazarin actually governs France. The Prince of Condé wins a major victory that breaks Spanish power at Rocroi on 19 May.
1646	King's Musketeers disbanded on 30 January by Cardinal Mazarin.
1648–52	Victory by the Prince of Condé at Lens in August leads to Treaty of Westphalia, ending the Thirty Years War, the treaty being signed on 24 October 1648. Revolt (called 'Fronde') of the Paris Parliament against Mazarin's government in late August. The Queen and the ten-year-old king flee the Louvre for safety on the night of 5-6 January 1649, an occasion that affected Louis XIV profoundly. Revolt (or 'Fronde') of the princes in 1650 as civil war rages; Condé goes over to the Spanish and occupies Paris in July 1652, but most rally to the regency to end anarchy. The young king and the court make a triumphant entry into Paris on 21 October, marking the end of the 'Fronde' revolts.
1650	Cardinal Mazarin raises his own guard company.
1653–59	Anglo-French alliance against Spain in April 1653. Louis crowned king on 7 June 1654 but most real power remains with Cardinal Mazarin. Marshal Turenne crushes Spaniards at the battle of the Dunes near Dunkirk on 14 June 1658; peace is signed on 7 November 1659. The Prince of Condé is pardoned.
1657	King's Musketeers raised again on 10 January by Louis XIV, who also becomes its senior captain. Actual command is devolved to the captain-lieutenant.

1660	Cardinal Mazarin turns his guard company over to the king.
1661	Cardinal Mazarin dies on 9 March; Louis does not appoint a successor and assumes full powers. In the years to follow, royal control becomes complete in all aspects of government.
1665	Louis XIV appoints himself as captain of the 2nd Company of the King's Musketeers.
1667–68	War of Devolution. French army invades Spanish Flanders. Holland, England and Sweden form an alliance against France.
1669	French contingent that includes a detachment of the King's Musketeers fights the Turks in Crete.
1672–78	Franco-Dutch War. England, at first an ally of Louis XIV, makes a separate peace in February l674 while Spain, Austria and some German states form an alliance with the Dutch against the French.
1681	French occupation of Alsace and Casale.
1683–84	War of the Reunions against Spain.
1685	Revocation of the Edict of Nantes on 22 October. All Huguenots to become Roman Catholic but many flee France.
1689–97	War of the Augsburg League. Austria, Brandenburg-Prussia, Holland, Piedmont, Sweden, England and Spain against France.
1702–14	War of the Spanish Succession. France, Spain and Bavaria against most of Europe.
1715	Death of Louis XIV on 1 September. He is succeeded by his five-year-old great grandson who becomes Louis XV. A regency and later Cardinal Fleury rule the kingdom until 1743.
1733–38	War of the Polish Succession.
1744–48	War of the Austrian Succession. France, Spain and Prussia against Britain, Austria, Holland and some German and Italian states.
1756–63	Seven Years War. France, Austria and Russia against Prussia, Britain and some German states. Russia changes side in 1762 while Spain joins a defeated France and tries to invade Portugal, but to no avail.
1774	Death of Louis XV on 10 May 1774. His grandson becomes Louis XVI.
1775	The King's Musketeers ordered disbanded on 15 December 1775, effective from 1 January 1776.
1814–15	The two companies of King's Musketeers are recreated on 15 June 1814 and disbanded on 31 December 1815.

Cardinal Richelieu about to inspect his guard, *c.*1629. Print after Maurice Leloir. Private collection. (Author's photo)

THE KING'S MUSKETEERS: THE UNIT

When a young man entered a career in the army in 17th- and 18th-century France, he was joining the largest and, in the opinion of many, the most modern army in Europe. Indeed, France at that time was the most highly populated country in Europe with an estimated 20 million inhabitants. By comparison, the Austrian empire would have had some eight million, Spain about seven million and Britain barely six.

The French army during the reign of Louis XIII was a relatively small force of about 50,000 men, guards included. Louis XIV greatly increased the army as soon as he took power in 1661. Six years later, it had 125,000 men and stood at about 200,000 men a decade later. In the war-torn 1690s and early 1700s, up to 450,000 Frenchmen were in army uniform. In peacetime, it would amount to about 200,000 men and, in times of war, up to half a million. It included the King's Musketeers as part of the *maison militaire* (or guard units) in the *maison du Roi* (the royal household).

The royal *maison militaire* consisted of the elite units of the army. During Louis XIII's reign, the guard units were divided into the *Garde du dedans du Louvre* (guard serving inside the Louvre palace) – the Gardes du Corps, the Cent-Suisses, the Gardes de la Porte and constabulary units serving on foot mostly as palace guards usually armed with halberds and partisans. The *Garde du dehors du Louvre* (guards serving outside the Louvre palace) included the other units. From the reign of Louis XIV, uniforms were introduced so that units were also grouped into the *Maison Bleue* (blue household) and the *Maison Rouge* (red household), named after the colour of their coats. Of the cavalry troops, the *Maison Bleue* consisted of the Gardes du Corps (bodyguards or lifeguards) that originated in the 15th century. The *Maison Rouge* was made up of the Chevau-légers (raised in 1593), the Gendarmes (1611), the King's

King Louis XIII and Cardinal Richelieu at the beginning of the siege of La Rochelle, September 1627. A King's Musketeer is nearby. Print after A. de Neuville. Private collection. (Author's photo)

Musketeers (1622 and 1657) and the Grenadiers à cheval (1676) until these horse grenadiers changed to blue coats in 1692.

In late 1622 according to Puységur's memoirs, Louis XIII's army was putting down disturbances in southern France. Following the occupation of Montpellier in late November or early December while the army marched towards Avignon, the king totally reorganized his guard Carabins by changing the rifled carbines to *mousquets* (matchlock muskets). The change from rifled to smoothbore muskets may have been because of the latter's faster rate of fire, but what the king wished to have was a new guard unit. He appointed new officers – the Sieur de Montalet was its captain – and called upon gentleman volunteers to form what was really a totally new unit: the Mousquetaires du Roi (the King's Musketeers), which had an establishment of 100 men. The new guard unit was to serve both mounted and on foot and be proficient with swords as well as muskets. Its troopers were preferably young men from the less wealthy provincial gentry who would gain a military education during their service in the company.

This company served in Paris near the palace of the Louvre where the royal family usually stayed. They were, du Verdier stated, 'on guard only when the king goes out and then they march two by two in front of all other guards'. In effect, they had actually gained precedence over other guard units when Louis XIII went out of the Louvre. The King's Musketeers were renowned for their outstanding bravery in combat and for their celebrated 'encounters' with Cardinal Richelieu's Guards. The king liked his guard musketeers and, on 3 October 1634, proclaimed himself their captain while appointing the Count of Tréville (also called Troisvilles) as the company's captain-lieutenant and commander. Eventually, Richelieu passed away in December 1642, followed by Louis XIII in the May of the next year. The King's Musketeers had now lost their protector; in early 1646, Cardinal Mazarin wished to pass command of the unit to his nephew the Duke of Nevers, but de Tréville flatly refused to go. Seeing this, the cardinal, who was also prime minister, disbanded the company on 30 January 1646.

The King's Musketeers had obviously left a favourable impression in the minds of many to the point that, ten years later, rumours ran high in Paris that 'their re-establishment is expected any day' according to du Verdier. It actually came on 10 January 1657 with the king as its nominal captain and, naturally, Philippe Mancini, Duke of Nevers, as the new captain-lieutenant of the 100 men of the re-formed King's Musketeers. As before, they served mounted and on foot, and again wore their famous blue cassocks with the silver cross. The company's precedence was to rank after the Gardes du Corps, the Gendarmes and the Chevau-légers of the guard because these were older units. Its strength quickly increased to 150 men and, by 1663, had doubled to 300.

Meanwhile, in 1660, Cardinal Mazarin had ceded his own personal foot guard company to the young King Louis XIV, who incorporated this hundred-man unit into his royal guard. In 1663, the king ordered the company henceforth to serve mounted as well as on foot for an expedition in Lorraine. At the end of 1664, he totally reorganized the company on the same footing as the King's Musketeers and, when he appointed himself as its captain on 9 January 1665, it officially became the 2nd Company of the King's Musketeers. The older 1st Company was nicknamed the *grands* musketeers or the *mousquetaires gris* (grey musketeers) because of the colour of their horses, while the 2nd Company was the *petits* (small) nicknamed *mousquetaires*

The Cardinal's mass, siege of La Rochelle, 1627–28. Every morning, those troops not deployed in the siege lines convened at Cardinal Richelieu's mass. The King's Musketeers, of course, had to be prominent attendees. Print after Maurice Leloir. Private collection. (Author's photo)

noirs (black musketeers) again on account of their horses. Initially, the 2nd Company was a less flamboyant corps, at least in terms of its dress, but, by the 1670s, it was equal in all respects to its sister company. In terms of protocol, the 2nd Company had precedence over the more senior 1st Company, but it was to become equal in other respects. Louis XIV was seemingly amused when, in 1680, his grandson the young Duke of Burgundy wanted to be a King's Musketeer. This brought about heated competition between the two companies over which he would join and thus show that the chosen company was the better since it had royal favour. The king solved the issue with something of a 'Solomon's judgment' by having the duke serve alternately in both. Getting the duke two uniforms was a small price for Louis XIV to pay in order to preserve his guard musketeers' unflinching loyalty and satisfaction.

Louis XIII and Cardinal Richelieu look on as the French army attacks Piedmontese positions in the mountainous Pas-de-Suze area on 6 March 1629. The King's Musketeers are unseen because they formed part of the 'forlorn hope' that overran the enemy defences. Print after Maurice Leloir. Private collection. (Author's photo)

'The Éminence Grise', c.1630. François Leclerc du Tremblay was a Capuchin monk who exerted considerable power by being the main adviser to Cardinal Richelieu. Painting by J.-L. Gérome. Boston Museum of Fine Arts. (Author's photo)

From 1665, each company was commanded by a captain-lieutenant, a sub-lieutenant, an ensign and a cornet and six *maréchaux des logis*. Each company then had some 300 men; this was reduced to 250 in 1668 and, thereafter, the strength of each musketeer company generally hovered around the same number of officers and men. There were also *brigadiers* (the rank of *brigadier* in the French cavalry was the approximate equivalent of a senior or first sergeant), 16 *sous-brigadiers* (a *sous-brigadier* was about equivalent to an infantry sergeant), an *enseigne* (this was a standard or colour bearer that had non-commissioned rank), six drummers, four *hautbois* (the *hautbois* were musicians that played a flute), a commissioner (supply official), a chaplain, a *fourier* (roughly translated as a quartermaster sergeant), a surgeon, a pharmacist, a farrier, a saddler and three treasurers. This then came to some 280 officers and men and each company was subdivided into four to six company-like squads. In 1693, the king added a sub-lieutenant, an ensign and another cornet. There were many variations thereafter, especially during the reign of Louis XV. For instance the number of non-commissioned officers (most of whom were really junior officers in status) was reduced. Thus, in 1747, each company had 176 men plus its seven officers, ten *maréchaux des logis*, four *brigadiers*, 18 sous-brigadiers, four *hautbois*, six drummers, ten *petits officiers* (aspiring officers) and a chaplain for a total of 231 officers and men. As can be seen, a company of the King's Musketeers could be as numerous as an ordinary line cavalry regiment on peacetime establishment.

While most of the two companies were lodged in Paris, a detachment was also posted at Versailles from 1682 when the king moved to this new palace. There, as before, a musketeer in full uniform and wearing boots went to see the king before he attended morning mass to enquire if he had any special orders. In the evening, before the king retired for the night, a musketeer officer would call on the king again to receive his orders. These were usually to do with escort duties, but might also concern highly sensitive and utterly secret state matters. When on campaign, both companies accompanied the king and lodged or camped on both sides of his tent or quarters. They furnished his escort with other guard corps when he went out and posted sentries at his door. When the king travelled in a carriage, the senior Garde du Corps troops were at its side with the guard Chevau-légers in front and the guard Gendarmes behind, but four King's Musketeers led the way in front.

The 1622–46 King's Musketeers had both trumpeters and drummers since they served mounted and on foot. A trumpeter had been appointed in 1657 when the corps was re-raised, but, in about 1663, he was replaced by five drummers and a fifer, all serving mounted. In 1665, three *hautbois* were added in both companies, later increased to four, while the fifer was replaced by a sixth drummer. A King's Musketeer, it must be recalled, was considered a foot soldier as well as a mounted soldier and thus the corps had, like the horse grenadiers, its allocation of drummers that also served mounted as well as on foot. The King's Musketeers did not have kettledrummers. As can be seen in the illustrations, their drummers had infantry-style drums that are said however to have been smaller, no doubt for convenience when playing mounted, and their beat 'was much more jaunty' than for ordinary drums.

In wartime, it was the practice to incorporate as many qualified *surnuméraires* as could be accommodated in both companies. The number of these supplementary King's Musketeers was variable, but might reach as much as a hundred men per company. Naturally, this was a superb opportunity for an ambitious young nobleman from the humbler provincial gentry to join the vaunted King's Musketeers and their commanders would be deluged with letters of recommendations when war broke out. While hostilities lasted, the *surnuméraires* were paid when the companies were on campaign, but this ceased when peace came and they each then had to wait until there was a vacancy in the corps. For encouragement, ten were admitted as *petit officiers* with some pay until vacancies opened.

At a higher level, an officer's commission in the King's Musketeers was *vénale* (it had a monetary value) and prices could be very high. In 1672, a cornet's commission went for 100,000 pounds, but prices could fluctuate and Joseph de Montesquiou, Count d'Artagnan (a distant relative of the famous d'Artagnan) obtained a commission in 1684 for a mere 40,000 pounds. According to the Duke of Saint-Simon, a renowned courtier who had been a King's Musketeer himself in his youth, when Count d'Artagnan acquired the rank of captain-lieutenant of the 1st Company in 1716 from the Marquis de Maupertuis (then over 80 years old), he had to fork out some 150,000 pounds. That year, an attempt was made to curb speculation by fixing the price of a cornet's commission at 60,000 pounds, but prices continued to vary; during the 1720s, the prices of commissions rose from 40,000 to 150,000 pounds. Some commissions were never offered on the 'market' at all. For instance, from 1716, the Monboissier family held the rank of captain-lieutenant of the 2nd Company and the commission was passed on to suitable family members for several generations. As can be seen below, when compared with the appointments of senior officers, these extraordinary amounts bore no relationship to their pay and they obviously had to have a significant private income.

A troop of mounted guardsmen, c.1630–35. They are probably men from the King's Musketeers since the official at left appears to be King Louis XIII with his retinue. Detail from a pen and ink rendering by S. Leclerc. Anne S. K. Brown Military Collection, Brown University Library, Providence, USA. (Author's photo)

RECRUITMENT

During the reigns of Louis XIII, Louis XIV and Louis XV, a recruit into the King's Musketeers was most likely to have come from the countryside, from one of France's provinces. At that time, about 85 per cent of the population lived outside cities; this meant that an aspiring young guardsman was likely to have originated from an old chateau or a manor house. The royal court might have been dominated by the immensely wealthy 'grand' noble families, but the vast majority of the nobility and the gentry were of more humble means and most lived on their estates, which usually provided their only income; they were not allowed, by law or society, to engage in commerce. If they did not remain on the land, and many could not, two basic career choices remained: the church or the army.

In his novels, Dumas made *cadet de Gascogne* (cadet from Gascony) a celebrated expression to denote the ambitious young gentleman seeking his fortune by his wits and, occasionally, by the skilful use of his sword. This somewhat romantic expression also reflected the grim social reality of most recruits, however ancient their titles may have been. To be a *cadet* in the family meant one would not inherit the estate; that went to the eldest son and few estates could afford to support more than one son living in the manner of a gentleman.

INSPECTING A RECRUIT IN THE KING'S MUSKETEER, c.1625–30

For a young country gentleman, being admitted into the King's Musketeers brought about a total change in lifestyle from that he had led at home. Undoubtedly, he would already have learnt the basics of sword fencing, musket firing and riding, and these were now to be much improved by sword, drill and horse masters. Quite apart from his letter of recommendation, he also needed to be physically very fit, agile and strong, as well as an obviously bright and quick-thinking young man. This was no unit for the meek or slow witted. Most of all, a recruit entering the King's Musketeers was in many cases just a mere teenager of about 17.

The plate shows a newly admitted young musketeer with his matchlock musket. His blue cassock bearing the cross hides a bandolier and charges that would most likely have been carried underneath. This was for infantry duty. Swords, the musketeer's primary weapon of choice, rather than muskets seem to have been used for mounted combat. The onlookers are, of course, older and more experienced members of the unit, present to tease and educate the newcomer in the peculiar world of the King's Musketeer. This young man will soon face untold dangers and adventures within a unique unit whose *esprit de corps* is still legendary. Alexandre Dumas summed it up best: 'All for one and one for all!'

King Louis XIII escorted by his musketeers at the surrender of Corbie on 15 August 1636. The cassock bears the cross, which has lilies at the ends of the arms and a faintly discernable sunburst at the centre. Detail from a contemporary engraving. Private collection. (Author's photo)

During the reigns of Louis XIV and Louis XV, a candidate wishing to enter the King's Musketeers had to be fit to bear arms and be at least 16 years old. This minimum age limit could be lowered by royal consent, as for ten-year-old Louis Balthazar de Girardot in 1750, but, on the whole, the average age of admission was 17, which was markedly younger than in other guard units; this was because the King's Musketeers also operated as a military academy.

Contrary to widespread belief, there was no formal requirement for 'quarters of nobility' as there was for entry in the Gardes du Corps or the guard Chevau-légers. A son from more humble gentry or from common stock, with the education and means to 'lead a noble lifestyle', could also be admitted. Indeed, from the late 1650s, Louis XIV insisted that only a 'person of substance' could be admitted to the King's Musketeers, that is to say a young man whose family fortune could support the expense of serving in the corps. In practice, it seems that sons of serving or former musketeers or sons of officers who had been made knights of the Order of Saint-Louis (created in 1693) were typical recruits into the corps. A long-serving and deserving King's Musketeer of humble birth might even ask for letters of nobility, such as M. de Grandchamp in 1737, who had served '18 years and whose father had been *maréchal des logis* ... and had served 44 years' or, in 1753, M. Fraissy de Veyrac, a veteran of 22 years in the 2nd Company.

Letters of recommendation were all-important and these appear to have carried considerable weight upon the acceptance of recruits in both companies. Dumas's *Three Musketeers* had d'Artagnan arriving in Paris bearing a letter of recommendation from his father to de Tréville, commandant of the King's Musketeers, and this is borne out in reality. Family relations were important and a young prospective musketeer was likely to show up with a letter of attestation from a relative or friend already serving in the corps. The father of the Duke of Saint-Simon did much the same as d'Artagnan's father in Dumas's novel when he wrote to 'his good friend' Captain-Lieutenant Maupertuis of the 1st Company recommending his son to him. Indeed, if accepted into the unit, a young musketeer was quite likely to serve with another family member. For instance, George Moneron de la Buissière, who was a *brigadier* in the 1st Company, helped no less than five of his young nephews to enter the King's Musketeers. The *brigadier* of the 2nd Company, René Claude de Girardot, Sieur de Launay, managed to have his seven sons enter the company as well as four of his grandchildren. One of his daughters married a musketeer so there can be no doubt that this was very much a King's Musketeer family in the days of Louis XV. Thus, and contrary to Dumas's novels that basically portray a musketeer as a lone adventurer with few and distant family ties, a real musketeer was very likely to find a family member standing in the ranks with him.

TRAINING

Novels and the cinema give the impression that a King's Musketeer was invariably a born expert in swordplay, an excellent horseman, a mature man in his late 20s or early 30s, wise to the ways of the world, possessed of a very good education, having impeccable manners and serving in the corps for most of his life. As seen above, a real 17th- and 18th-century musketeer arrived in the corps as a teenager of about 17. He would of course already have basic writing, reading and mathematical skills, and have some knowledge of history, science and geography. He may well have had private lessons by a sword master and be a proficient horseman. Unlike the portrayal in the cinema and novels, a musketeer was subject to a gruelling regime of frequent drills and parades. These would occur both on foot as

A King's Musketeer, c.1635–40. The cassock has the usual cross with lilies at the ends of its arms and flames at the centre. The lower arm of the cross is slightly longer than the others. Note the musket fastened to the front of the saddle with its barrel hanging on the trooper's left side. Print after J. Callot. Private collection. (Author's photo)

infantry and also mounted as cavalry so that a musketeer had to master both infantry drill with musket and sword, and cavalry drill with the sword. The drill was stringent and every musketeer had to appear in best dress, especially as the king might happen to come by.

King Louis XIV never missed inspecting his musketeers at least once a year. Indeed, during the late 1650s when a teenage king, he loved to conduct drill in the inside open court of the Louvre palace. Since the king knew the drill very well and was a stickler for details, every musketeer was almost terrified that something might go wrong during a royal inspection. And sometimes it did. In his memoirs, the politician Mirabeau recalled an incident involving his grandfather as a teenage musketeer during one of the king's inspections, seemingly in the 1680s. His shoes being too tight, he had slit them, but now found that his scarlet stockings 'contrasted strongly with his shoes'. The young musketeer 'got some ink and, thinking he had blackened his stockings, had in fact only made a dark red spot. The king arrived and the troubled young man put the heel of his right foot on top of the spot on his left foot [to hide the mark]. Louis XIV, attentive [to details] and in all of his pomp stopped and said: "Musketeer, you are not [standing] properly under arms." The musketeer had to assume the proper position and this drew [all eyes] to the faulty spot; and the whole [of the king's] suite burst out laughing as much as their master's majesty would permit.' This young musketeer's career was not affected and he went on to become a general.

Another soldier who had served as a young musketeer in Louis XIV's days was the Duke of Saint-Simon and he was critical of the educational regime in place for the King's Musketeers, feeling that 'it abused the young nobility in a barbaric way' because a young musketeer was reduced to performing drill like a common private trooper and a private grenadier. In fact, instilling discipline into proud and cocky young noblemen was part of

the curriculum; an excellent way to do this was to submit them to stringent drills. Veteran soldiers were on hand to help so that, after a period of time, the young musketeer in training with his companions would become a well-trained and disciplined trooper.

Sons of officers were traditionally admitted as cadets in French army units to learn the rudiments of military life in army camps and on campaign. The 1622 King's Musketeers had some of the elements of a military school, but it was during its second raising that it became more like a military academy. Various courses on literature, history, sciences and the arts were given by professors. This corps was the only place where the art of war could be studied in depth and it was widely believed that one had to be a King's Musketeer for a successful military career. After two years of service in the corps, a young musketeer was deemed to have acquired enough knowledge and training to buy a captain's commission, usually in a line infantry regiment. If the family was of more humble means, a lieutenant's commission in the line could nevertheless be granted to a deserving young musketeer and, like many of his comrades, he might go on to have a brilliant career.

Drummers of the King's Musketeers, c.1640. Being mounted infantry, the unit had both drummers and trumpeters. Print after Marbot based on Della Bella. Canadian War Museum, Ottawa. (Author's photo)

 DRESS OF THE KING'S MUSKETEERS, c.1657–64

When the King's Musketeers were re-established in January 1657, they again wore a blue cassock with white cross, made famous by the exploits of the 1622–46 unit. The plate here shows what a musketeer might have looked like when he took part in the fighting of the late 1650s, such as the 1659 battle of the Dunes or at the arrest of General Controller of Finances Nicolas Fouquet in 1661.

There was no uniform as we understand it at that time, but some uniformity was achieved with livery garments. For a King's Musketeer **(1)** this meant wearing a cassock that identified him as a royal guard. This was the famous blue cassock lined with red, edged with silver lace and bearing on its front, back and side panels the badge consisting of a white cross with lilies at the end of its arms and sunburst at its centre. The details, however, are unclear because of the paucity of sources and the various possible interpretations of the existing descriptions. For instance, it is not certain if the lilies were gold or silver although gold seems to be favoured. The sunbursts at the centre are usually assumed to be red for the oldest company, but some descriptions mention gold, which could also be interpreted as a reddish-gold hue, especially if gold as well as red silk thread was used. The edging of silver lace may have been single or possibly double. Descriptions mention ciphers, but these remain unknown and are possibly seen only on exceptional dress occasions during the 1660s. The rest of the clothing was the musketeer's own and followed the latest fashions.

A musketeer's sword was likely to be a rapier still, but this was being replaced by the 'musketeer-style' sword that featured a brass hilt and a sturdy and wider straight blade **(2)**. A matchlock musket **(3)** was also carried and the holsters on the saddle held a pair of pistols **(4)**.

1

2

3

4

Graham Turner '13

CONDITIONS OF SERVICE

Charles de Batz de Castelmore d'Artagnan, c.1670. He is shown in armour holding a baton, the symbol of military command. There is no certainty that this likeness is faithful, but it is the only known portrait of the famous musketeer. Frontispiece of the 1704 Amsterdam edition of the memoirs by Courtiz de Sandras. (Author's photo)

The lifestyle of a King's Musketeer was generally befitting that of a young gentleman. Each had at least one servant, who had usually come with him from his home province and who was likely to have been well known to his family. He would look after the needs of his young master and also take care of his horse.

During the 17th century, the King's Musketeers were lodged in homes and inns near the Louvre palace. Their horses were quartered in various nearby livery stables. Louis XIV felt a better arrangement had to be made and he had two 'hotels' (or rather, well-appointed quarters) built in Paris to lodge them, as well as adjoining stables for their horses. One was built in 1707 for the 1st Company on du Bac Street in the district of Saint-Germain. It consisted of an elegant three-storey building with a large inner court. The building for the 2nd Company, constructed in 1708 on Charenton Street in the suburb of Saint-Antoine, was even larger since it had four storeys and contained some 340 rooms with fireplaces, so each musketeer had heating in his room. Both were spacious and each had equestrian arenas and parade grounds to practise horsemanship and foot drills. All subalterns and musketeers were required to lodge and sleep in these quarters. Permission had to be obtained from the company's captain-lieutenant to do otherwise. A detachment of four musketeers served and slept at the stables under the command of a *brigadier* or a *sous-brigadier* whose duty was to ensure that the horses were in good health and well cared for. This service was carried out in rotation and no musketeer could be excused from it; each and every musketeer had to be a good and attentive horseman. Indeed, it would seem that every one of them loved horses. From the time the king moved to the palace of Versailles in 1682, a detachment was permanently posted there and, from 1689, it lodged at the 'Hôtel de Limoges' on de Sceaux Avenue near the palace's gate. It would have used the superb equestrian arena of the nearby royal stable. Any musketeer from that detachment was free to wander at leisure in the palace's superb gardens and hallways when not on duty.

When on campaign, a musketeer would often lodge at the home of a local inhabitant, who, in theory, had to provide a room with two wide beds, one for two musketeers, another for two servants and room in the stable for two horses. This might produce conflict; the musketeer expected decent lodgings for him and his servant while the host family coped with this major intrusion in its home. The general perception regarding the quartering of military men in a private home is usually that they would invade the place and would probably steal or damage property; if the owners complained, they might be roughed up or worse. But records reveal otherwise. In 1730, the musketeers lodged in Nemours. There, the Marquis de Chiffreville, ensign in the 2nd Company, complained that the widow Le Roy had not allowed him to use the kitchen, the dining room and a 'cabinet' and had further filled her stable with barrels rendering it unusable. Another officer, the Viscount of Canillac, mentioned that his host had refused to give a room to his servant, yet his home had more than enough rooms. Other homeowners did not assign rooms with fireplaces and the officer responsible for lodging finally reported that the 'majority of musketeers are obliged to sleep two by two and most in beds that are barely three feet wide'.

A musketeer standing guard at the palaces had *bouche à la cour*, which meant he was fed from the royal kitchens. In 1638, the musketeer's daily ration consisted of two loaves of bread and a pint and a half (0.75 litre) of wine. On campaign in the 18th century, he was allowed two loaves of bread weighing two pounds (one kilo) each, two pints of wine, two mugs of beer or cider and half a pound of beef or veal or lamb. More specifically, a party of four officers and 60 musketeers escorting the king on campaign ate 15 pieces of lamb, 15 pieces of veal, 12 pieces of 'lard' (ham) and 10 of poultry daily, as well as a loaf of bread and a pint of wine per non-commissioned and private musketeer. Fish replaced meat on Fridays

and other 'fish days' prescribed by the Roman Catholic Church. An officer could further enjoy salads, a fruit plate and a baked pastry. All this would cost 123 pounds for meat days and 131 for fish days for this detachment. All in all, a King's Musketeer ate and drank quite well and some of this food might also have fed his servant. There was other food that could be purchased in addition, and the option of dining at local inns.

The pay of a King's Musketeer was far higher than a military man in a line regiment, as was the case for all guard units. According to the 1748 *État général des troupes de France*, a captain-lieutenant received 8,400 pounds, a sub-lieutenant 1,200 pounds, an ensign 900 pounds, a cornet 900 pounds, a *maréchal des logis* from 450 pounds, a *brigadier* 585 pounds and a *sous-brigadier* 535 pounds, an *hautbois* 900 pounds, a drummer 453 pounds, a chaplain 450 pounds and one of the ten 'small officers' 378 pounds. A private musketeer would have 498 pounds. This basic pay was augmented by a food and horse forage allowance that added another 2,511 pounds to a sub-lieutenant's appointment and 716 pounds to a musketeer's, to make a total of 3,711 and 1,214 pounds respectively. When one compares this with the line cavalry at the time, one sees that a King's Musketeer was far better off. A line cavalry lieutenant-colonel received 561 pounds basic pay annually plus another 1,864 pounds for food and forage while a line trooper had 79 pounds plus a 447-pound food and forage allowance making 2,425 and 526 pounds respectively. These figures could vary in detail and circumstances, but seem to have been fairly standard during the reigns of Louis XIV and Louis XV. This may seem excessively generous, but belonging to the guard was expensive. A musketeer had to defray the expense of his uniform, his sword, his pistols, his equipment, his horses and horse furniture. The king provided only the cassock (later *soubreveste*) and muskets. There was also the expense associated with having at least one servant. On the whole, by the 1740s, it was recommended that a prospective musketeer should have a private yearly income of about 1,500 pounds plus be prepared to spend an equivalent amount on at least one horse, uniform and equipment before even considering an application to enter the King's Musketeers.

A young musketeer was reputedly very rowdy off duty. Cinema has projected a vision of a relatively mature musketeer indulging in 'wine, women and song', but a high proportion of King's Musketeers were in their late teens. If any parallel can be made, it might be with the 'adventures' and pranks of just about any high school or college student of our day. A young

Escorting the king and important officials was one of the duties of the King's Musketeers, as shown here, in about 1645. Print after Jacques Onfroy de Bréville (better know as JOB). Private collection. (Author's photo)

'Wine, women and song' could be the title of this tavern scene showing some of the levity that was certainly practised enthusiastically by young musketeers in the St-Antoine district in Paris… and probably elsewhere as well. The subject was supposed to be 'The Prodigal Son amongst harlots' painted in 1637 by Johan Baeck who, to make it socially acceptable, turned it into an episode from the Bible in order to portray events familiar to many a patron of a tavern. Kunsthistorisches Museum (Fine Art Museum), Vienna. (Author's photo)

musketeer undoubtedly considered himself a 'student prince' about to conquer the world, or at least to conquer the petticoat of a comely young lass at one of the many taverns near his quarters. And he could certainly muster enough pocket money to have a fine time. This rowdy life appears to have been especially prevalent during the reign of Louis XIII, but certainly did not vanish later, the accounts of following reigns frequently mentioning *jeunesse débridée* (wild youth) among the King's Musketeers.

DUELLING WITH THE CARDINAL'S GUARD

During the Middle Ages, challenging an opponent to a duel was the way a gentleman would settle personal issues, with the assistance of 'God's judgment'. In spite of the disapproval of the Church, the practice carried on into the 16th century at which time fencing with rapiers became very popular. At a time when the slightest perceived insult was cause for a duel, sword fights between gentlemen became rampant in France; up to 10,000 men may have perished in duels between 1588 and 1608. It had become a scourge; many a gentleman, who could have put his sword to better use fighting the nation's enemies, died pointlessly. Thus, King Henri IV forbade duelling in 1609, but this was largely ignored. On 24 March 1626, King Louis XIII, encouraged by Cardinal Richelieu, signed another edict forbidding duelling on pain of the guilty gentlemen losing their commissions in royal service as well as their pensions if caught. On that very day, which was Easter Sunday, François de Montmorency, Count of Bouteville, a notorious swordsman who had fought some 20 duels, ignored the edict and slew yet another opponent on a busy Paris street. This was too much for king and Church. He was caught and, as a warning to others, condemned and beheaded. Duellists were thereafter careful to be discreet, choosing isolated spots to fight and being treated in secret if wounded. Indeed, it seems the real-life musketeer Athos died from duel wounds in 1643.

What then of the famous sword fights between the King's Musketeers and Cardinal Richelieu's Guards? They certainly occurred, perhaps almost constantly, and were looked upon as something of a sport by both the king and the cardinal rather than individual duels. Typically, small groups of musketeers and guards would run across each other on a Paris street and, after a few cat calls, swords would be drawn and a sword fight would ensue. This is what is shown in our plate. Just the sight of the blue and red cassocks must have been a signal to the people on the street to stay clear; however, watching a fight – officially called a 'meeting' – was tolerated by the highest authorities in the land. Thus, the King's Musketeers and Cardinal's Guards of the 1620s and 1630s enjoyed royal tolerance when it came to swordplay in the streets.

Louis XIV felt he had to put a stop to these fights and duels. In 1655, he declared his resolution to 'abolish this pernicious practice in my kingdom'. His successive edicts were widely applied and this spelt the end of duelling as a fashionable practice. Being a King's Musketeer in the time of Louis XIV or Louis XV was very different from the free-wheeling times of Louis XIII.

A sword fight on the Pont-Neuf (new bridge) in central Paris, c.1660. Detail from an unsigned contemporary painting. Musée Carnavalet, Paris. (Author's photo)

PARTICULAR SERVICES

In 17th- and 18th-century France, every important official and influential nobleman was allowed a unit of his own personal guard. Every guardsman was employed to watch over his master's safety, but he played an even greater role in asserting his master's authority and prestige. He might be part of a unit that numbered only a couple of dozen men; the guard company of a governor general of a province or a colony usually numbered about 20 officers and men. The higher the official, the larger his bodyguard would be. In this respect, the very powerful Cardinal Richelieu had few equals because of the importance and prestige of his station. In a sense, he ruled France during the reign of King Louis XIII. As a result, his 'Cardinal's Guard' was the largest and best guard unit in the realm, apart from the royal guards. From 1626, following a failed assassination plot, the king authorized Richelieu to have a guard of up to 100 men led by a captain, a lieutenant, an ensign and six sergeants, all of which had to be gentlemen rather than the ruffians portrayed in the cinema. Louis XIII further allowed the Cardinal's Guard to have 200 musketeers serving on foot in 1632. Some 60 of the mounted Cardinal's Guard were on duty every day to ensure the safety of their master. The usual disposition of these troops was that the cardinal always had a company of infantry on guard outside his residence and more bodyguards inside his residence and near his person.

There were indeed many swashbuckling incidents that took place between the Cardinal's Guards and the King's Musketeers. King Louis XIII was known sometimes to have difficulty enduring his most brilliant statesman. For his part, Cardinal Richelieu combined a fear of assassination with a tinge of noble pride in pomp and circumstance. Thus, to appear everywhere with a body of his own guards considerably enhanced his personal safety as well as giving him a certain standing and prestige second only to the king himself. In any event, the great cleric-statesman was increasingly ill and his guard was disbanded following his death in December 1642. His designated successor, Cardinal Julius Mazarin, became the prime minister of France in 1643 and retained the post until 1661, although much contested and scorned. He also had his own guard unit. It appears to have been initially less numerous, but it was reported to be 300 guards on foot in 1658, a number that may be somewhat exaggerated. In 1660, Cardinal Mazarin gave his guard unit to the king, who accepted it, eventually turning it into the 2nd Musketeer Company.

Cardinal Richelieu's Guards wore red cassocks bearing a white cross on the chest, sides and on the back. Some renderings show the cassocks edged with yellow lace. In 1658, Cardinal Mazarin's Guards were described as wearing a red cape, on which his coat of arms was embroidered. Other guard units of the time also usually wore cassocks in the colour of their masters' livery. During the 1640s, the Duke of Elbeuf's guards had green cassocks edged with silver and white silk Lorraine crosses, while the Duke of Bouillon's guards had white and black cassocks and the Duke of Beaufort's had scarlet cassocks with white silk crosses having a lily at the end of each point. In 1661, to name just a few, the governor of Paris's guards had yellow cassocks with white crosses, with a white sunburst at the centre; those of the Duke of Epernon had green cassocks with white crosses; the queen's bodyguard had red cassocks. Even in faraway French America, its governor general between 1664 and 1667, the Marquis de Tracy, was allowed by King Louis XIV – and this was a rare privilege – to have his 20 guards wear similar cassocks to the King's Musketeers. Indeed, the nursing nuns of the Quebec General Hospital wrote that he never went out in public without being escorted by part of his guard led by its captain, four pages and a group of officers. Such was the dignity expected from a high official of the crown. In 1744, the Prince of Conti impressed courtiers with his guard of 50 gentlemen 'well equipped and well mounted' and dressed in yellow laced with silver thread.

The King's Musketeers moving on campaign, c.1664. Detail from a painting by Adam van der Meulen. Musée Lambinet, Versailles. (Author's photo)

However, for any aspiring young man from the gentry or nobility, the *nec plus ultra* was to be admitted into the King's Musketeers. Along with select members of the Garde du Corps, King's Musketeers were the only type of guardsman entrusted with extremely delicate and utterly secret missions from the king himself.

Secret agent

All three of Alexandre Dumas's novels, as well as Courtiz de Sandras's apocryphal memoirs of d'Artagnan, are largely concerned with secret service missions and discreet arrests of powerful individuals by officers of the King's Musketeers, assisted by detachments of their men. But, in reality, would a King's Musketeer actually be involved in the 17th-century version of covert operations?

The answer is yes. As the Duke of Saint-Simon recalled, it was known at court that musketeers were specially designated to make arrests and guard important prisoners. The royal guard comprised two units that were more involved in this type of operation: the Garde du Corps and the King's Musketeers. Officers and men in both units had blind loyalty and absolute respect for the sovereign. The personal safety of the royal family was their first and most sacred duty. Furthermore, they had to be most efficient in carrying out whatever missions, public or confidential, asked of them.

Members of the young, lively, blindly loyal and thus discreet King's Musketeers created in 1622 became ideal candidates for such covert operations. The France of Louis XIII was also going through a thorough transformation largely owing to the far-seeing policies being introduced by Cardinal Richelieu. In terms of real authority, he was second only to the king. One of his most trusted and feared advisers was François Leclerc du Tremblay (1577–1638), also known as Father Joseph, and most famously the 'Éminence Grise'. His nickname was due to his grey friar's habit worn by the Capuchin Order. As Richelieu's agent, he went on to become one of the most powerful individuals in French diplomacy. Naturally, King Louis XIII very much resented Richelieu's power while supporting the wisdom of his policies that made France the most powerful state in Europe. Nevertheless, as seen in Montglay's memoirs, ill feelings were such at court that Richelieu feared being assassinated by some crazed sword-wielding member of the king's guards in a palace corridor.

Novels, memoirs and, from the 20th century, cinema on the subject of the King's Musketeers invariably depict them in a series of seemingly never-ending duels – presented as full-scale street and tavern battles – that would have cowed any group of local constables attempting to stop them. Sure enough, much of this can be verified. Contemporary writers of the period

APPROVAL OF A NEW UNIFORM, 1688

The king, being the senior officer of several royal guard units, was responsible for various administrative duties and one of these was the procurement of uniforms. King Louis XIV was especially diligent in these duties and required to see a guardsman wearing a uniform with the proposed new features. The King's Musketeers appear to have been of particular interest to the king and he often made his wishes known with regard to their appearance. The plate represents the introduction of the new sleeveless *soubreveste* in 1688, which reduced the problems associated with the cassock, which had become almost cloak-like over the years and quite cumbersome. This must have been of special interest to the king, who furnished the cassock and the *soubreveste* at his own expense. Thus, a musketeer was brought to see the king wearing the proposed new garment for his approval before it was made.

Beneath the new *soubreveste*, the young musketeer wore his scarlet uniform. The coat was generously adorned with bunches of blue ribbons, as was still the fashion at the time. It was decorated with gold lace indicating that this musketeer belonged to the 1st Company. His hat was also laced with gold and also had an elegant border of white plumes as well as a white ribbon cockade. The belt was laced with gold and, on the sword, the guard was gilded. Except for having silver lace, buttons and sword hilts, the 2nd Company had the same type of uniform. A musketeer was armed with the traditional matchlock musket and a sturdy broadsword with the *à la mousquetaire* hilt that became almost universal in all armies by the end of the 17th century.

Guard of the Governor General of New France and the French West Indies, 1644–68. By royal permission, the Marquis de Tracy's guard company was dressed the same as the King's Musketeers and it was armed with rifled carbines. Watercolour by Michel Pétard. (History and Heritage Directorate, Department of National Defence, Ottawa)

agree that there was much rivalry between members of the King's Musketeers and the Cardinal's Guards that erupted into full-scale insults whenever they ran into each other off duty. Swords were drawn and 'combats very often' fought. The king delighted when hearing that his musketeers had bettered the Cardinal's Guards, while Richelieu would applaud when his guardsmen had run off the King's Musketeers.

The problem was that duels were forbidden anywhere in the realm. Furthermore, such behaviour by some of the kingdom's best swordsmen and soldiers went against all precepts of military discipline. But, in this case, the application of law was relaxed and some major fight would occur on a weekly basis. These fights were condoned as 'meetings' by the royal and episcopal authorities – to do otherwise would have involved a major deployment of police-like troops and the prisons would have been filled weekly with guardsmen belonging to the king or to the cardinal awaiting trial. Both parties did not wish anything of the sort because both the king's and the cardinal's guardsmen were involved in covert activities. There seems to be no precise information about what these were at the time of Louis XIII, but Alexandre Dumas may not have been too far off the mark in his depiction of the dark world of plots involving his musketeers in the late 1620s and 1630s.

A clue to a musketeer's dabbling in covert activities is that, even after the first establishment of the King's Musketeers was disbanded in 1646, d'Artagnan was kept on duty by the wily Cardinal Mazarin. He now served as 'one of the gentlemen of His Eminence' according to the *Gazette de France* on 30 June 1646. The maze of secret missions and discreet interventions in the next decade is beyond the scope of this small book. Suffice it to say here that d'Artagnan became a trusted confidant and messenger to Mazarin, the queen mother and young King Louis XIV in the times of deep turmoil called 'La Fronde' that saw separate revolts, first by the parliamentarians of Paris and then by some of the leading noble families. D'Artagnan was reputedly a good swordsman and there can be little doubt that such talent must have come in handy to fight off those who tried to intercept him, the messenger, in a dark alley or an isolated stretch of road.

When the King's Musketeers were re-raised as a guard unit in January 1657, d'Artagnan, who had a commission as captain in the Gardes Françaises, was upgraded in May 1658 to a lieutenant's commission in the company of the King's Musketeers. This may sound like a demotion, but it was in fact a promotion to something like lieutenant-colonel in the army. On 9 March 1661, Cardinal Mazarin passed away, un-mourned by both the people and the king. All courtiers assumed that Mazarin's passing away would give them more power. Louis XIV, who had always been kept away from real influence, now played his hand to seize absolute autocratic power. He first declared that, from then on, he would personally assume the mantle of prime minister and leader of the government. Not only would he reign, he would also rule.

From 1653, Nicolas Fouquet had been the kingdom's general controller of finances, a sort of super finance minister, and he had made extensive use of his position for self-enrichment. He had political friends and allies in all circles and was extremely well informed. But Louis XIV was also taking note of Jean-Baptiste Colbert, who certainly had more ability than Fouquet in financial matters. Fouquet had built an opulent residence at Vaux-le-Vicomte, still one of the finest chateaux in the region of Paris, and there lavishly entertained a deeply affronted young king; it seemed that Fouquet, the servant of the state, had more power and wealth than the king. Thus, Colbert's suspicions that public funds were being diverted en masse to Fouquet's private and secret coffers were confirmed in the king's mind. Worse, the king's spies reported that Fouquet had even discreetly acquired the fortress at Belle-Isle, of which he was already governor, for himself and had privately paid for work on its refurbishment. A safe haven in case things went wrong? Whatever Fouquet's motives were, Louis XIV resolved that he had to go. Easier said than done. Fouquet was politically a very powerful man and any move against him might erupt into civil war.

Louis XIV thus planned what amounted to a secret *coup d'état* to remove the outlandish Fouquet. In theory, the king could have asked the commander of his Gardes du Corps to arrest him. But, at this time of great intrigue and secret agreements, the king knew that the commander of the Gardes du Corps was a friend and follower of Fouquet. One can easily surmise that the general controller of finances would discreetly reward the Gardes du Corps commander, and possibly some of his fellow guardsmen too, for relaying to him some of the important secret matters they heard at the royal court. Thus the king could not trust his own life guards. Should they hear that some secret plot was afoot regarding Fouquet, he would soon hear about it and the whole operation would collapse. Yet, to take power, Louis XIV simply had to have Fouquet arrested.

To achieve this, the king called upon possibly the most experienced man when it came to intrigues and secret missions, d'Artragnan, from his company of musketeers. On 4 September 1661, the king made his move and signed the *lettre de cachet* that instructed d'Artagnan to arrest Fouquet. Louis XIV and his cabinet ministers were then at Nantes to inaugurate the États de Bretagne, as the legislative assembly of Brittany was called. A relatively quiet cabinet meeting had been planned and Fouquet was

The knight's cross of the Royal and Military Order of Saint-Louis, 1698. This medal, which comes with the coveted honour of a knighthood, was awarded to Philippe de Rigaud de Vaudreuil (*c.*1643–1725), who started his successful career as a King's Musketeer in 1672. Appointed commandant of the troops in Canada in 1687, his capacity for diplomatic and administrative work was revealed and he was named governor of Montreal in 1699 and, four years later, promoted by the king to be the governor general of New France. Many other musketeers also had successful careers and received similar honours. De Vaudreuil was promoted commander in this knightly order in 1712 and awarded an honorary grand cross in 1721. Château de Ramezay Museum, Montreal. (Author's photo)

Each musketeer had at least one servant. In this print after Maurice Leloir, the lackey 'Mousqueton made a very good figure when attending his master' the musketeer Porthos of Alexandre Dumas's *The Three Musketeers*. Private collection. (Author's photo)

A jolly gentleman and a comely girl singing a duet, c.1623–24. 'Men made their way in the world by the means of women without blushing. Such as were only beautiful gave their beauty… Such as were rich gave, in addition, part of their money' wrote Alexandre Dumas of the 17th century in *The Three Musketeers*. Painting by Gerrit Van Hornthorst. Montreal Museum of Fine Arts. (Author's photo)

to be discreetly apprehended once he had left by the gates of Nantes Castle and put into a heavily escorted carriage that would take him to the castle at Angers to be detained. The main worry was that Fouquet might slip away and escape to the fortress of Belle-Isle, from where he could put up stiff resistance and possibly start a civil war.

D'Artagnan was probably the only musketeer aware of the plot. As was the custom, when the king travelled, his musketeers provided much of his escort. At Nantes, the whole company was there. As a King's Musketeer, escorting the travelling sovereign was part of ordinary duties but things now became truly extraordinary. The king's secret instructions specified that d'Artagnan would detach 40 musketeers from the company, posting half in the courtyard and half outside the gates of Nantes Castle. D'Artagnan was to be accompanied by 'five or six [musketeers] that would always be with him'. When the cabinet meeting ended, Louis XIV retained Fouquet for a few minutes to look at documents so that when the general comptroller of finances finally came out of the castle, he was alone. D'Artagnan and his musketeers were about to move in when one of Fouquet's friends showed up and they went on to Nantes. When informed, Louis XIV icily responded that d'Artagnan had to find and arrest Fouquet. Accompanied by a squad of musketeers, d'Artagnan soon spotted Fouquet alone in front of the cathedral on his way to his residence in Nantes. Fouquet had no idea that he was being pursued when he was surrounded by the King's Musketeers. D'Artagnan handed him the *lettre de cachet* and asked an ashen-faced Fouquet to come with him, first to a nearby house in order not to draw too much attention to the situation, and then into the special carriage that came to collect him.

One may wonder what an ordinary King's Musketeer who took part in this extraordinary arrest thought. Certainly, he must have felt privileged to participate in such an operation. Although certainly not fully understanding what was going on, he knew that something outstandingly important was going on and, better still, that he was part of it. It further proved that the king had the highest trust in his musketeer's ability, bravery, loyalty and discretion. This last point was important. No one was to know just where Fouquet would be taken. The carriage had steel blinds and was escorted by a hundred of the King's Musketeers. Inside sat Fouquet, d'Artagnan and a few more musketeers. The remaining detachments of the King's Musketeers were posted on the main roads out of Nantes with orders to arrest any courier trying to get to Paris. One of Fouquet's valets actually did get through, but it

The musketeer's secret service duties, c.1670. A detained gentleman (at right) in discussion with a legal official in a setting that could be almost any castle that held important state prisoners. His servants are bringing drinks and setting the table for his visitors. An officer stands nearby. This later 19th-century painting was inspired by an episode in the last of Alexandre Dumas's musketeer novels, *The Vicomte de Bragelonne: Ten Years Later*, which dealt with *The Man in the Iron Mask*, which is also the title of this unsigned canvas. The officer in the blue coat appears to represent Captain d'Artagnan or d'Auvergne de Saint-Mars. Chateau Laurier Hotel, Ottawa. (Author's photo)

was too late. While Fouquet's carriage was travelling to Angers Castle, a three-day journey, police and guard detachments took over his Paris houses looking for compromising papers while ten companies of Gardes Françaises and three companies of the Swiss Guards appeared at Belle-Isle and took over the fortress.

Thus did Fouquet's world crumble in an instant by the king's will and at the hand of his trusted guard musketeers. From Angers Castle, he was transferred to the castle in Vincennes, near Paris, until again transferred to the Bastille in June 1662. There he was detained during his trial, which dragged on until December 1664. Unsurprisingly, the court found him guilty of embezzlement and of diverting state funds. He was condemned to perpetual exile and his properties were seized.

When presented with this judgment, Louis XIV was not satisfied. Exile was tantamount to Fouquet's release and left him free to plot against the French crown in the safe haven of a neighbouring

The King's Musketeers at the siege of Maastricht during June 1673. This detail from a mural, apparently painted shortly after the event, shows several mounted King's Musketeers. This adorned one of the halls of the Invalides, which now house the Musée de l'Armée in Paris. Although much damaged by time, these latest restorations reveal ample blue cassocks under scarlet cloaks. This might be portraying members of the 1st Company as the lace is gold and the horses are grey, but this is not certain. (Author's photo)

An officer of the King's Musketeers at the siege of Ghent, 1678. He wears a scarlet cloak over his cassock. Note the multi-branched gilt-hilted sword. Detail from the later 17th-century mural painting of the siege of Ghent. Musée de l'Armée, Paris. (Author's photo)

country. Instead, the king ordered he be jailed in France for the rest of his life. During his detention, he was guarded by a detachment of the king's most trusted guardsmen: his musketeers. D'Artagnan was in charge and permanently had a strong detachment of his men with him. All were ordered to reside in the same castle where the prisoner was detained. The watch was permanent and, when relieved, the musketeers were to lodge and sleep in the same area of the castle where Fouquet was held. The castle itself was secured and repairs made as necessary. For example, the somewhat rickety castle received a new gate and an iron grille was even installed in the fireplace in Fouquet's room. At Vincennes and the Bastille, the 45-man detachment of the King's Musketeers and their officers literally took over these castles because their mission was considered so important that their ordinary garrisons of jailers and governors were kept away. Access to such an important state prisoner was only through a few musketeers and their officers were required to sleep next to his room. Even the chaplains Fouquet requested were carefully selected.

This watch duty by a number of the King's Musketeers went on until January 1665 when Fouquet was transferred to the fortress of Pignerol, at the foot of the Alps (now Pinerolo in Piedmont, Italy). D'Artagnan and his men were at last relieved. The King's Musketeers' senior non-commissioned officer (but actually an officer in the army) Benigne d'Auvergne de Saint-Mars was henceforth posted at Pignerol with a company of infantry. As for Fouquet himself, he passed away at Pignerol in 1680. But from 1669, Saint-Mars had another prisoner, later to be famous, the very mysterious 'Man in the Iron

Two troopers of the King's Musketeers at the siege of Ghent, 1678. Both hold their carbines and are about to go into action. The musketeer at left appears to have folded back his large cassock revealing its scarlet lining; the one at right has a scarlet cloak over the cassock. Detail from the later 17th-century mural of the siege of Ghent. Musée de l'Armée, Paris. (Author's photo)

Mask', who was not just a fictional character. Practically nothing is known of this prisoner, least of all his true identity; his secret movements from various prisons are documented to some extent and it seems that his mask was worn for health reasons, only when he went out. Whoever he was, the 'Man in the Iron Mask' passed away at the Bastille in 1703, taking his secret with him.

Delivery of a *lettre de cachet* with a short stint as prisoner's guard was the usual kind of secret duty that a King's Musketeer might expect. A musketeer officer was, after all, the last official to see the monarch at night and he might have to take 'orders' from the king. Of the more famous persons later arrested, one could point to Lieutenant-General Antoine Nompar de Caumont, who was apprehended for unknown reasons by officers of the Garde du Corps in November 1671. With Fouquet removed, the life guard was again considered trustworthy. Nevertheless, the duke was turned over to a detachment of 100 King's Musketeers under the command of d'Artagnan who then brought him to the fortress of Pignerol, where he was detained until released in 1681. Charming as ever on his return to court, he was forgiven by the king, commanded the French contingent to Ireland in 1689 and, in 1692, was made Duke of Lauzun. American readers might be interested to learn that this Duke of Lauzun bore no relation to the famous commander of Lauzun's Legion at the 1781 siege of Yorktown. De Caumont had no children when he died in 1723, but the title of Duke of Lauzun was recreated in 1766 for Armand-Louis de Gontaut-Biron who fought in the American War of Independence.

These famous arrests on the secret orders of Louis XIV certainly had an effect on the good behaviour of courtiers at Versailles and other royal residences. A Garde du Corps or a King's Musketeer was never far

A trooper of the King's Musketeers, *c.*1695. Detail from a print after N. Guérard in his *Les Exercices de Mars* published in Paris. Anne S. K. Brown Military Collection, Brown University Library, Providence, USA. (Author's photo)

A King's Musketeer, early 18th century. Print in Father Daniel's 1722 *Histoire de la Milice Françoise*. (Author's photo)

away, but one does not get the sense that this was regarded as oppressive. To be a nobleman whisked away by a musketeer certainly put an end, for a time at least, to a courtier's career. However, the torture rack was not the next stop. There was no rough treatment and everything was carried out politely. Noblemen and churchmen, as a rule, were not tortured, as this was considered most uncouth and only reserved for commoners. A closely guarded apartment at the Bastille or at the Fortress of Pignerol was certainly not a 'spa', but neither was it a sordid cell. Comfort depended on the status and means of the prisoner and the better off would have servants, good food and wine, appropriate furniture and so on. The punishment consisted of loss of liberty and contact with the outside world.

KING'S MUSKETEER UNIFORMS, WEAPONS AND SADDLERY, 1740s

Figure (**1**) shows a musketeer of the 1st Company. He wears the unit's blue *soubreveste* edged with silver lace bearing the company's distinctive cross that has three red flames in the corner of each quadrant at the centre. Beneath was the scarlet uniform coat, the sleeves and cuffs of which are visible as well as the bottom of the skirt, which was slightly longer than the *soubreveste*. The waistcoat and breeches were also scarlet. The buttons and lace on the coat and waistcoat were gold for the 1st Company. The hat was embellished with white plumes and its brim was edged with gold lace. The cockade could be white or black; it was not until 1767 that the cockade was ordered to be white only throughout the army. The buff belt was edged with gold lace and the guard of the sword was gilded. The gloves were light buff and the boots were black leather.

Figure (**2**) shows the back view of a *brigadier* of the 2nd Company. The *soubreveste* and the scarlet uniform are almost identical to those of the 1st Company. However, the *soubreveste*'s cross has five sunburst flames in each quadrant at the centre; the lace and buttons were silver instead of gold; the sword hilt was silver plated. The *soubreveste* of a *brigadier* had three rows of silver edging lace. A *maréchal des logis* (not illustrated) had four silver laces as well as the king's cipher embroidered in silver at the bottom of the *soubreveste*'s skirt.

Both figures are shown on foot, but about to mount their horses. They wear boots with spurs and gloves, and are armed with swords and muskets. The sword is the classic *à la mousquetaire* type with its heavy and straight blade (**3**). The musket's exact appearance is unknown. A 1741 order for 400 muskets for the King's Musketeers reveals that this musket barrel was 108.28cm long, had a flat lock and counter lock, that its butt plate had a 'tail' 12.1cm long, that it had swivel rings (one held by its own barrel band) and that there was a thumb piece engraved with the cross or possibly a flaming grenade, and its ramrod had a horn tip. It seems to have had up to four ramrod pipes and did not have barrel bands other than for the sling swivel. The musket's sling was most likely of dark red Russian leather. There seems to have been no cartridge box until about 1750 (the illustration shows a cartridge box from the 2nd Company), but there was a powder flask, seemingly covered with leather, slung across the shoulder with a blue cord. It should be noted that a King's Musketeer *maréchal des logis* did not carry a musket since he had officer status. The pair of pistols kept in the saddle holsters of each musketeer was steel mounted and marked with the names of their respective companies. In the middle of the 18th century, the pistol had a total length of 57.4cm, barrel length of 39cm and was 16.7mm calibre (**4**). There may have been slight variations on later orders, but, on the whole, the pistols appear to have remained the same until 1775.

The type of saddle (**5**) used by the cavalry of the guard, roughly from the 1620s to the second half of the 18th century, was the *à la royale* (royal) type, which basically called for a dark red Russian leather padded seat, sometimes covered with velvet, fitted over a wooden form. It initially had a front pommel that had been gradually eliminated by the 1730s to prevent accidental injuries. A girth went under the horse to fasten the saddle. Underneath the saddle was a padded saddle blanket and the housing (or *schabraque*), with steel stirrups hanging down on leather straps at each side. The leather pistol fonts (or holsters) attached to the front of the saddle had cloth covers. For the King's Musketeers, the saddle blanket and font covers were scarlet, edged with gold or silver and also featured a gold or silver cord and tassels, a practice peculiar to the musketeers. The cloak-like blue cassock could be carried fastened behind the saddle, usually rolled so that its scarlet lining was on the outside. In the mid-18th century, the harness and bridles were made of black leather.

MOUSQUETAIRES DU ROY.
2.ᵉ Compagnie.

King's Musketeer *brigadier*, *sous-brigadier* and standard-bearer of the 1st Company, 1724. The *brigadier*'s cassock was edged with five narrow rows of silver lace, the *sous-brigadier*'s with four narrow rows of silver lace. Print after Delaître. Private collection. (Author's photo)

APPEARANCE – UNIFORMS, COLOURS AND STANDARDS

The King's Musketeers are universally known by their blue cassock lined with scarlet and edged with silver lace. The cross on the front, back and sides was a white fleurs-de-lis and flames at the centre. From this, a great many variations were invented by modern costume designers and numerous illustrators, who varied the colour of the cassock from light to dark blue, sometimes even with a violet tinge, and created endless versions of the cross. This was not just a result of artistic licence, but also because there is practically no detailed information about the early cassocks of the King's Musketeers. Early prints and paintings, some of which are reproduced in this book, occasionally show the cross to have a slightly longer lower arm. Possibly the earliest written description appears in the 1642 *État de la France* that states the King's Musketeers 'wear blue cassocks distinguished with silver crosses'. Sieur du Verdier's 1656 *Le vray et nouveau estat de la France* confirmed that 'they all had blue cassocks with a silver cross'.

Late in January 1657, Philippe de Villers noted that each musketeer 'had a blue cassock with large silver crosses that had gold lilies at the ends [of its arms] and flames [at the centre]. The whole cassock is edged with silver lace.' In 1660, the King's Musketeers escorting the royal couple's entry into Paris were described as follows: '… the first 76 [musketeers] had sprays of white plumes [on their hats]; the 72 that followed had white, yellow and black plumes; the plumes of the third troop, formed by 52 [musketeers], were white, blue and black; and finally those of the last 60 were white and green'.

They were mounted on white horses, wore their blue cassocks and were said to be much more richly dressed than the other companies and had 'crosses with lilies at the end of the arms, the ciphers and crowns, all embroidered in gold and silver'.

In April 1665, Father Sebastiano Bocatelli observed the musketeers parading at Pré-aux-Clercs near Paris. The first company, or 'Grand Musketeers', was described as being:

> well mounted on fine-looking horses that were almost all white or mottled white and grey. They [the musketeers] all wore blue cloth cassocks edged with silver lace and with a cross on the back and the chest surrounded by a sunburst that was embroidered with gold and the king's cipher... Their cassocks... were worn over very handsome blue cloth coats decorated with silver embroidery. The housings of their horses were of *zinzolin* [violet] with four suns embroidered in silver at the four corners... They had very fine plumes on their hats. Their companions, the [2nd Company or] Small Musketeers... were mounted on *moreaux* [black] horses appointed similarly to those of the Grand Musketeers; but they did not have the double silver lace [on their cassocks] and their clothes under [the cassocks] were of ordinary cloth. Their horse's housings were blue with a crowned L. They also had very fine-looking [hat] plumes. Their muskets, shined like those of the Grand Musketeers... None can enter the musketeers unless he is a gentleman, and the rivalry that exists between the Grand and the Small Musketeers is the reason that they always wear the latest fashions and clothing of extravagant richness.

Drummers, King's Musketeers of the 1st (left) and 2nd (right) companies, 1724. Watercolour by Lucien Rousselot after Delaître. Anne S. K. Brown Military Collection, Brown University Library, Providence, USA. (Author's photo)

Two years later, the King's Musketeers escorted the king entering the captured city of Tournai wearing their 'blue cassocks laced with silver' and buff jackets.

In the early 17th century, cassocks were relatively short and reached the thighs. From about 1660 they became more ample, thus somewhat assuming the appearance of a cloak. It appears that each side panel was fastened with small buttons. These large cassocks became increasingly cumbersome. Louis XIV decided to correct this situation and, in 1688, ordered that the cassock would henceforth be replaced with a *soubreveste*, which could be described as a sleeveless coat. It was blue, edged with silver lace, and had a cross on the chest and on the back. It appears that, at least from that time and probably earlier, the King's Musketeer's cross was of white velvet edged with silver lace and had gold lilies at the end of the arms of the cross. At the centre (corners) were three scarlet flames for the 1st Company and five 'aurore' (orange) flames for the 2nd Company. The *soubreveste* remained the same until 1776, subject only to changes in the cut in order to conform with fashion. From the

Standard of the 1st Company of Musketeers, 1724. Print after Delaître. Private collection. (Author's photo)

Standard of the 2nd Company of the King's Musketeers, c.1750–75. Musée de l'Armée, Paris. (Author's photo)

mid-18th century, its skirts could be fastened back to form scarlet turnbacks.

From 1688, both the *soubreveste* and the long cassock were issued, the latter being used as a cloak. The musketeer was henceforth issued with both items at the king's expense. Beneath the cassock or *soubreveste* a steel cuirass would be worn so that it remained invisible. This cuirass was procured at the expense of the musketeer as it was in the Gardes du Corps and the Gendarmerie. It seems that a King's Musketeer had a sort of love–hate relationship with this cumbersome item, but nevertheless had to have it.

Until the middle of the 17th century, a King's Musketeer dressed in his own clothes. Recognition was achieved by means of cassocks and of sashes. From the 1660s, uniforms were introduced and, while a musketeer was still responsible for procuring his clothing, which was traditionally quite luxurious, royal wishes now had to be taken into serious account. When Louis XIV wanted his musketeers to be especially splendid, he might order them to be dressed uniformly. Once, Father Daniel later recorded, the king requested they wear buff suits and the wealthiest musketeers embellished these with quantities of diamonds fastened on their sleeves. Another time, the king ordered black velvet to be worn. In 1665, as seen above, they had blue coats embroidered with silver. Thereafter, the two companies each had a distinct uniform that remains undocumented. Following the 1673 siege of Maastricht, the king ordered that both companies would wear the same uniform, the 1st Company's being laced with gold thread and the 2nd Company's with silver. However, the *État de la France* of 1680 mentions the 2nd Company with 'silver and gold' lace but only silver again from the 1690s. In 1677, the uniform was scarlet and it remained so until the companies were disbanded. There was no facing colour; the whole coat, cuffs and lining included were scarlet, as were breeches and waistcoats.

Initially, a King's Musketeer wore heavy cavalry boots when serving mounted. However, in 1683, Louis XIV ordered lighter boots to be worn, with a fixed spur; they were eventually replaced by boots that were semi-rigid, to make walking easier. When the king was travelling, a musketeer would mount guard booted.

Nothing is known of the standards and colours of the 1622–46 musketeers. From 1657, the King's Musketeers were unique in the army in that each company had both a cavalry standard and an infantry colour since they served as both mounted and foot troops. Both flags had similar ornaments, embroidered on the standard and painted on the colour (see illustrations). If they paraded and fought mounted, only the standard was displayed and, if on foot, only the colour was unfurled.

EQUIPMENT – WEAPONS, ACCOUTREMENTS, HORSES

When the first King's Musketeers appeared in 1622, there were no regulation model weapons and an early musketeer was armed with a variety of swords and firearms. Only matchlock muskets were carried by the King's Musketeers, until about the end of the 17th century when flintlock carbines were distributed to NCOs only and, eventually, to all musketeers. But tradition dictated that matchlock muskets were the formal weapons to be carried at parades; flintlock carbines were to be used only on campaign. Pairs of flintlock pistols were probably added during the 1660s. It should be noted that NCOs and officers were armed only with swords and, when on duty, on foot, with halberds and spontoons respectively.

The charge of the King's Musketeers with the royal household cavalry at Fontenoy, 11 May 1745. This detail from the huge battle painting by Pierre L'Enfant painted later that year shows the King's Musketeers with blue cassocks and red coats. Their senior officers in front wear scarlet coats. Musée de l'Armée, Paris. (Author's photo)

The early swords would have been rapiers. Possibly as early as the 1650s a sword model called *à la mousquetaire* appeared, the elegant-looking brass guard of which featured a single knuckle bow, a *pas d'ane* curling to the *ricasso*, below which was the counter-guard. For cavalry troopers, the sturdy and straight steel blade could be some 90cm long. This model became the nearly universal type of sword used in the French army from the reign of Louis XIV. A lighter version was also used by infantrymen. The origin of its *à la mousquetaire* name is unknown. The hilts were gilded for the 1st Company and silver plated for the 2nd Company.

Towards the last years of the Seven Years War, a new and very attractive sword model was adopted by both companies. It had a flat straight blade of some 92cm long and its guard had a knuckle bow with a shell to protect the hand better. The guard was gilded for the 1st Company and silver plated for the 2nd Company. Its pommel had a cross with three flames for the 1st Company and five flames for the 2nd Company. The blades were engraved with the King's Musketeers' cross and '1re' or '2me compagnie des mousquetaires du roi' as well as *De la marque de la Mouchette à Solhingen* and, finally, on the flat edge of the blade *Giverne Md fourbisseur Rue Vieille Boucherie à L'Épée Roÿale à Paris*, indicating where the swords were assembled. This model remained until the corps was disbanded.

From the reign of Louis XV, only flintlock muskets with bayonets were carried, but the models remain unknown as no actual example appears to have survived. As for pistols, the early types must have varied from the 1660s, but, later on, their style was fairly similar to those carried by the Gardes du Corps.

The early King's Musketeers had shoulder baldrics for their swords, worn under the cassocks, until replaced by waist belts from about 1683. They were of buff leather edged with gold or silver lace and buckles. Contemporary artwork does not show a bayonet frog and scabbard, so this may have been fixed to the saddle. For many years, the cartridge box was put in the right pistol holster and a powder horn slung over the shoulder with a narrow buff belt, edged with gold or silver lace. From about the late 1740s, a shoulder cartridge box was carried. It had a Russian leather flap featuring the cross at its centre and laced with gold or silver; its belt was of buff leather edged with gold or silver.

The housings of the early King's Musketeers are unknown, but may have been blue or violet. The 1677 *État de la France* mentions that the 2nd Company had silver lace by then. The housing's colour was later changed to scarlet. The saddles and bridles were in the French style with yellow or white metal buckles according to the company. A leather pocket hung below the right pistol holster to rest the butt of the musket.

The horse, which was to be at least 14 hands, was bought by the individual musketeer and was to cost 300 pounds. Initially, there was no uniformity regarding the colour of horses used by a musketeer. In 1660, they had white horses. From 1665, by order of the king, the 1st Company was mounted on white or light grey horses and the 2nd Company on black horses.

King Louis XV and his staff at the battle of Fontenoy, 1745. An escort of the King's Musketeers can be seen in the background on the left. Print after Alphonse de Neuville. Private collection. (Author's photo)

A musketeer of the 1st Company, *c.*1745–50. Contemporary unsigned portrait. Musée de l'Armée, Paris. (Author's photo)

BATTLES

A King's Musketeer stood for one thing above all: a fighting man. From the first battles, every musketeer gained an outstanding reputation for utter bravery. Thus, a musketeer had a good chance of being wounded or killed, but the prospect of winning laurels at sword point was overwhelming, especially as a King's Musketeer was very often in his late teens or very early twenties – an age when a young man-at-arms thinks he is immortal.

Any campaign had its share of skirmishes and a King's Musketeer had to be very vigilant since he was part of the unit that ensured the king's security when he was with his army. But a King's Musketeer was not just a guardsman; he was often expected to attack at the very front of the troops. The first major engagement came as part of the long and complicated siege of La Rochelle in 1627–28. On the nearby fort on the Ile de Ré, the royal garrison was blockaded by Protestant troops and a relief force sent in. It included the King's Musketeers, which fought on foot in such an outstanding way that the enemy departed. The siege itself offered few opportunities for distinction. After La Rochelle's surrender, King Louis XIII and Cardinal Richelieu led the army east in 1629 to find the Pas-de-Suze blocked. Again, the king ordered his musketeers to be part of the 'forlorn hope' and this brilliant action is illustrated by one of our plates. Other actions followed during the last phase of the Thirty Years War.

Soon after they were re-raised in 1657, the King's Musketeers galloped off to northern France. As usual, outstanding bravery was the hallmark of every musketeer as the Spanish found when, in 1659 at the battle of the Dunes, the company repulsed four charges of enemy cavalry. The King's Musketeers participated in all the sieges of the War of Devolution and, at the 1667 siege of Lille, assaulted and took part of the fortifications within

PAS-DE-SUZE, 6 MARCH 1629

In a gesture of ill-placed pride, the Duke of Savoy objected that the French army should march through the narrow Alpine mountain pass called the Pas-de-Suze in Piedmont (Italy) to reach a Spanish army. Early in the morning of 6 March 1629, King Louis XIII decided to break through the pass, which was defended by a Piedmontese force of about 2,700 men. Its commander, the Count of Verrue, boasted that this time the French would not merely be dealing with the English as they had at La Rochelle. The pass was blocked by fieldworks that consisted of some 30 redoubts and two lines of barricades, each being 3.7m thick (12ft) and 6.15m (20ft) high. Louis XIII and Cardinal Richelieu were present and ordered their troops to attack, take the fieldworks and reach the town of Suze. A two-pronged assault on the flanks of the first barricade was planned. There were no uniforms at the time and, to help recognition, it is likely that the Piedmontese wore blue sashes and the French had white sashes, except for the musketeers who, because of their cassocks, would be instantly recognizable.

At six in the morning, the French and Swiss guard infantry and 48 companies of line infantry advanced towards the Piedmontese barricade. The king ordered that his musketeers should dismount and join the 120 *enfants perdus* (forlorn hope) of the French Guards so that over 200 guardsmen now advanced. They were formed into two squads to attack both flanks at the same time. They ran up to the barricade under fire, but never wavered. The defenders did not expect such a determined assault; while the forlorn hope of the French Guards went against the right flank, the King's Musketeers, led by Lieutenant de Tréville, overtook the left flank barricade, slashing at anything that moved. Within minutes, the enemy beat a retreat on both sides and the French supporting troops poured all over the fieldworks and, eventually, also gained possession of Suze's outer forts and, finally, the town itself. The king and Cardinal Richelieu were not far behind – indeed one of the cardinal's guards was killed by enemy fire. They saw it all; a King's Musketeer was extremely brave and fearsome in battle.

A musketeer of the 2nd Company, c.1745–50. Contemporary unsigned portrait. Musée de l'Armée, Paris. (Author's photo)

15 minutes. The town capitulated the next day and its governor was very surprised to see that most musketeers were only 17 or 18 years old. At Dôle in Franche-Comté the following year, about 40 King's Musketeers attacked and took an enemy outer fortification; seeing this, the Prince of Condé, who commanded the French army, swiftly ordered infantry to support him and the town surrendered the next day.

One of the more unusual services was Louis XIV's detaching a hundred of his musketeers with a force led by the Duke of Beaufort to fight the Turks at Candia on the island of Crete in 1669. Candia, a Venetian outpost, had been under siege or blockaded by the Turks since 1646 in retaliation for the capture by the Knights of Malta of a convoy that had been carrying part of the Sultan's treasure and harem when returning to Istanbul following the pilgrimage to Mecca. The deeply shamed Turks had vowed eternal revenge and, in 1669, some 40,000 Ottoman troops lurked outside Candia's walls. A call for assistance was made to all European courts and some answered, including Louis XIV. In June, a French fleet with 6,000 men arrived, but the Ottomans put up a stiff fight. Still the King's Musketeers' detachment drove off Turkish cavalry during a sortie, but at a cost of two killed and 32 wounded. The French relief force was beset with misfortune; the plague was rampant, a 58-gun French ship accidentally blew up and the Duke of Beaufort was killed in action. The sickly garrison's morale, now reduced to 3,600 men fit for service, was at a low ebb and, following the Turk's offer for all Christians to be free to leave Candia, the place capitulated on 27 September. A musketeer returning after such an adventure must have had a lot of exotic tales to tell.

In 1672, war was declared on Holland and the King's Musketeers crossed the Rhine on 2 June. In June 1673, the French army was besieging Maeastricht with the assistance of a British contingent sent by King Charles II. Present with the musketeers was Captain-Lieutenant d'Artagnan, while the young John Churchill – destined to become one of Britain's greatest generals – was with the British corps. The assault was made on a half-moon fortification. Lord Alington was in the thick of the fighting and left an account of what went on next:

> There was Monsieur Artaignan with his musketeers who did very bravely. This Gentleman was one of the greatest reputation in the [French] Army, he would have persuaded the Duke [of Monmouth] not to have past that place, but that being not to be done, this Gentleman would go along with him, but in passing that narrow place [d'Artagnan] was killed with a shot through his head, upon which the Duke and we past where Mr O'Brien had a shot through his legs.

A King's Musketeer of the 1st Company, *c*.1745–50. He wears his blue *soubreveste* over a scarlet coat and he rides a light grey horse, the mane and tail of which is decorated with scarlet ribbons. The colourist mistakenly made the lace on the *soubreveste* gold rather than silver, but correctly put gold lace on the hat, uniform and housings. Print after Eisen. Anne S. K. Brown Military Collection, Brown University Library, Providence, USA. (Author's photo)

A King's Musketeer of the 1st Company wearing a cassock, *c*.1745–50. Officially still called a cassock, this garment was actually a cloak, although it bore the unit's cross. Print after Eisen. Anne S. K. Brown Military Collection, Brown University Library, Providence, USA. (Author's photo)

A King's Musketeer cartridge box, 2nd Company, c.1745–50. Musée de l'Armée, Paris. (Author's photo)

The soldiers at this took heart the Duke twice leading them on with great courage; when his Grace found the enemy being to retire, he was prevailed with to retire to the trench, the better to give his commands as there should be occasion. Then he sent Mr. Villars to the King [Louis XIV] for 500 fresh men and to give him an account of what had past. When those men came, our enemies left us without any further disturbance, masters of what we had gained before the night. So that to the Duke's great honour, we not only took more than was expected, but maintained it after we had been in possession of it, but with the loss of a great many men and many brave officers. (TNA, SP, 78/137, quoted in Churchill's *Marlborough*).

The demi-lune was ultimately taken by a King's Musketeer charge and the city surrendered, but the great d'Artagnan was no more. Such was the hero's end, 'in the arms of glory', for the man that inspired Alexandre Dumas and it certainly befitted any real-life King's Musketeer.

The war continued with more sieges in Flanders and farther south on France's eastern frontier. In March 1674, Besançon was taken, following a daring attack by the King's Musketeers that secured a position on part of its fortifications. At Condé in 1676, both companies charged as the forlorn hope on the night of 25–26 April and broke through the defences and, followed by infantry grenadiers, penetrated the city, which quickly capitulated. The following year brought even more laurels to every musketeer, owing to extraordinary bravery at Valenciennes. This remarkable action is the subject of the plate opposite. Less than a month later, on 11 April 1677, the King's Musketeers were with the French army outside the city of Cassel facing the

G **ASSAULT ON VALENCIENNES, 17 MARCH 1677**

In the spring of 1677, Louis XIV's French army surrounded the fortress city of Valenciennes in Flanders. Marshal de Luxembourg arrived on the scene on 9 March when the siege trenches started to be dug on the north side of the city. The city was strongly fortified and it was thought that it would require a long and bloody siege to take it. At nine in the morning on 17 March, a first assault on the outer works was attempted by grenadiers of the guards regiments, the two companies of King's Musketeers and the Picardie Regiment. Attacking with their usual bravery and vigour, the musketeers soon managed to take the half-moon fort that dominated the other fortifications. Looking at the action from a distance, King Louis XIV was much surprised and pleased to recognize his scarlet-coated musketeers on the walls and in possession of the outer works. He was to be even more surprised. The musketeers now rushed a very narrow bridge over the moat, fought off its defenders, entered and took a half-moon redoubt at sword point. A number of musketeers of the 1st Company found another narrow bridge leading to a sally port and scattered its defenders, and the most daring went up a stairway while clearing it of enemy soldiers; they went up onto Valencienne's ramparts and then into the city. The enemy counter-attacked, but in vain. Each musketeer sought to establish a defensive position, some in nearby houses, others on the captured wall, while comrades of the 2nd Company arrived to reinforce them, soon followed by the guards and Picardie regiments who started to pour into the city. The rest of the French army came up to penetrate the breach. The city's governor capitulated to prevent rampage and pillage. It was an extraordinary feat and was brought about by the bravery of the King's Musketeers. Valenciennes was ceded to France by the treaty of Nimègue (Nijmegen, Holland) in 1678.

Colour of the 1st Company of the King's Musketeers, c.1745. Private collection. (Author's photo)

Colour of the 2nd Company of the King's Musketeers, c.1745. Private collection. (Author's photo)

Prince of Orange's infantry, which twice repulsed the French line cavalry. The King's Musketeers were called to renew the attack; they dismounted, charged on foot and broke the enemy line. The French infantry behind them caught up and finished the fighting while the musketeers coolly went back to their horses to await their next orders. The king's brother was present and reported that the two musketeer companies had opened the way to a victory. They also participated with distinction at the sieges of Ypres, Courtray, Philipsbourg, Mons and Namur.

After a few years of peace, war broke out again. In 1691, the King's Musketeers were called to attack the seemingly impregnable fortification of Mons. During that siege, each musketeer's eagerness to charge was such that, by the king's command, a musketeer who went forward before his line of comrades would be shot on the spot by his own lieutenant. The hostilities ended in 1697, but war was again declared in 1702. This time, the French armies were roundly defeated in Flanders by the Duke of Marlborough, who was ably assisted by Austria's Prince Eugene. Louis XIV's marshals were mediocre and it was only towards the end of the war that Villars emerged as a great general. For a musketeer, it was a grim time in spite of extraordinary courage. At Ramillies, on 20 May 1706, the King's Musketeers charged with the rest of the royal guard's cavalry and, at first, swept off four enemy lines. But Marlborough, taking advantage of Marshal Villeroi's tactical mistakes, now outflanked the French army and counter-attacked; in spite of the musketeers' and other guardsmen's desperate resistance, the French line infantry eventually broke and ran in panic. Oudernade, fought in 1708, was also a defeat. At Malaplaquet on 11 September 1709, the royal guard cavalry, including the King's Musketeers, charged Marlborough's cavalry four times and forced it to withdraw near its infantry. But, once again, tactical ineptitude eventually decreed a withdrawal of the French army.

A long period of peace followed the end, in 1713–14, of the Spanish War of Succession. The King's Musketeers were present at the siege and capitulation of Philipsbourg in July 1734, but were not involved in major operations until 1743 when deployed at Dettingen. Once again, enemy tactics proved superior and the *maison du Roi* found itself surrounded by British cavalry, the 2nd Company of the King's Musketeers being in the thickest fighting with a loss of 29 killed and 57 wounded, as well as losing a standard. For a surviving musketeer, it was a financial disaster because many horses and weapons were lost, all of which were paid for privately. But, as always, every musketeer fought ferociously; for instance, it took 15 sabre cuts and several shots to bring Maréchal des Logis Thésy finally down. During that engagement a famous incident occurred: King's Musketeer Philippe de Girardot de Malassis, wounded by a sabre blow to the head, lay unconscious when found by British soldiers who carried him to the Duke of Cumberland's tent. He was the son of King George II and had also been wounded by a shot in the leg but,

Trooper of the 1st Company of the King's Musketeers, *c.*1763. Note the skirt of the cassock that is now turned back. Watercolour by Pierre-François Cozette. (Author's collection)

seeing Girardot, he insisted that his surgeon should attend him first. Girardot eventually recovered. Field Marshal Darlymple, Earl of Stairs, further ordered that surgeons should attend other wounded guardsmen. Such humane and chivalrous gestures were occasionally seen during the 'lace wars' and, sadly, seem to have largely vanished since.

Two years later, the royal guard cavalry was campaigning again in Flanders under the eye of King Louis XV himself, of his son the Dauphin and of Marshal Maurice de Saxe commanding the French army. On 11 May 1745, they were at Fontenoy facing the Duke of Cumberland's allied army of British, Dutch and German troops. At last, fate smiled on the royal guard cavalry's legendary bravery and a great French victory was gained that day. It is the subject of one of our plates. The guard cavalry campaigned in Flanders until 1748. It was not deployed during the Seven Years War until 1761, when the King's Musketeers formed part of Marshal Soubise's army operating in the lower Rhineland. There were no notable engagements in what turned out to be the last campaign in which a King's Musketeer would participate. His valour in all battles, which often bordered on heroism, never wavered and was never in doubt. A King's Musketeer was the very incarnation of bravery in the heart of his countrymen and it earned the esteem of his opponents.

H   CHARGE OF THE MUSKETEERS AT FONTENOY, 1745

On 11 May 1745, during the War of Austrian Succession, a French army numbering about 50,000 men led by King Louis XV and commanded by Marshal Maurice de Saxe met an army of 53,000 Britons, Dutchmen and Germans under the command of the Duke of Cumberland in the vicinity of the village of Fontenoy in Flanders. The French had occupied the strategically important village of Fontenoy and the Duke of Cumberland resolved to take it. If Fontenoy fell, the French would lose the battle. Although they had a weaker force, the French had two positive factors in their favour; the presence of the king and his son, the 'Dauphin' (the crown prince of France), greatly boosted the army's morale and, secondly, Marshal de Saxe was one of the best military minds of his day. He was sickly and in pain, but his eyes and mind were sharp. Cumberland gathered his best infantry into a large column of at least 10,000 men that would sweep aside everything opposing it. The engagement started with a famous incident of Lace Wars bravado; when the French guard infantry came to face the British guards, the latter were invited to fire the first volley by their gallant opponents. The resulting British guards fire broke up the first French line and the British column advanced; French counter-attacks failed to halt it although Fontenoy did not fall. The ferocity of the fighting made the British column become more compact, but still it advanced and, by noon, it seemed nothing could stop it. However, the French regrouped a number of battalions and brought artillery to fire on the column; this was taking its toll on the concentrated mass of redcoats. A final blow was needed and the guards cavalry, up to then held in reserve, was now called upon to charge the enemy column. Needless to add that both companies of the King's Musketeers were present and that every musketeer was eager to charge.

Thus, sword in hand, the musketeer with his comrades and the whole of the guards cavalry advanced at a trot, a canter and, finally, a full gallop that crashed onto the column. This mass of cavalrymen was too much for the already weakened column; it stopped and started to waver. French infantry now joined in and the column at last broke; but its battalions rallied around their colours and its retreat was orderly. Again, every musketeer and, indeed, every royal guardsman had fought with outstanding bravery.

AFTER THE BATTLE

What happened to a King's Musketeer once he left his unit? Most general officers started their military lives in the King's Musketeers. The Baron of Beaupré was a young musketeer in the early 1640s who had risen to general when he was killed in 1679. The Viscount of Lautrec entered the 2nd Company in 1690, was noted as a bright young gentleman, became colonel of his own dragoon regiment in 1696 and, true to his musketeer's code of outstanding bravery, was killed in 1705 fighting at Brescia, Italy. The Baron of Champagne joined the 1st Company in 1741, was a general from 1759 and survived the wars. Some even served overseas. Young Philippe de Rigaud de Vaudreuil joined the marines, went to Canada and became the governor general of New France from 1703 to 1725. But perhaps the most famous expatriate was the young Gilbert du Motier, Marquis de La Fayette, who, after being a youthful King's Musketeer, joined the American army fighting for independence and became one of its better generals; he gained the esteem of George Washington and the gratitude of all Americans, then and ever since.

Trooper of the 2nd Company of the King's Musketeers, c.1770. Musée de l'Armée, Paris. (Author's photo)

MOUSQUETAIRE NOIR

However, a musketeer might also remain in the corps, usually as a non-commissioned officer, and retire after several decades of service. Alexandre Dumas, who was a well-known gourmet as well as a novelist, provides us with a final and charming look at a retired King's Musketeer who turned to gardening. He grew extraordinarily flavoursome peaches on his little estate near Montreuil north of Paris and had a favour to ask of the king. He was a friend of the king's director of gardens at Versailles who arranged for a basket of 'Montreuil peaches' to be served for the king's desert when he hunted nearby. The king was most pleased and wished to thank the gardener who accordingly showed up wearing his old uniform; the surprised king was even more delighted, granted the favour and also raised his old musketeer's pension on condition that he could have a basket of his sublime peaches every year. A wonderful royal tribute for a faithful old warrior.

IMITATORS

The reputation of the King's Musketeers was such that other rulers considered forming their own versions of this guard unit. In 1690, the Elector of Brandenburg Frederick William had his mounted Trabaten-Garde wearing blue cassocks with crosses on. This unit eventually vanished, but the fame of the King's Musketeers was still strong in Prussia decades later. Thus, in 1740, the Prussian Garde du Corps was raised as a guard cavalry regiment to be the personal bodyguard of the king and, from 1871, of the emperor of Germany. To be a member of this unit was to be at the very peak of German military society since a Garde du Corps served by the side of his monarch, just like a King's Musketeer in France. A scarlet *soubreveste* was worn over his white uniform (*supraweste* in German) with the star of the Order of the Black Eagle on its front and back. The unit was disbanded in 1918.

A senior Prussian adjutant, probably on his way to see King Frederick II (the Great), converses with an officer of the Gendarmes during the 1760s while a young Garde du Corps scrutinizes them quietly. This guard unit, similar to the King's Musketeers in France, was responsible for the king's safety and oversaw access to him. Inside the palace, the guardsmen wore an ornate scarlet *soubreveste* decorated with the star of the Order of the Black Eagle. Print after A. Menzel. Anne S. K. Brown Military Collection, Brown University Library, Providence, USA. (Author's photo)

The King's Musketeers of France also had imitators in Spain. From October 1702, King Felipe V of Spain raised a company of 100 musketeers to be part of his royal guard and dressed them in the same uniform as the 1st Company. It will be recalled that he was, as the Duke of Anjou, the grandson of Louis XIV who had been put on the Spanish throne thus causing the Spanish War of Succession (1702–15). The main difference between the King's Musketeers in France and their counterparts serving Felipe V was that, in Spain, musketeers did not attend a military academy, but were recruited mostly from veteran officers. Thus, a young but impoverished hidalgo was not likely to be found in the ranks and neither was an older gentleman; whereas in France both might well have

Officer and trooper of the Chevaliers Gardes of the Russian Imperial Guard, 1793. Their *soubreveste* was obviously inspired by that of the French King's Musketeers and even featured lilies at the ends of the arms of a Maltese cross. Contemporary print. Anne S. K. Brown Military Collection, Brown University Library, Providence, USA. (Author's photo)

been found amongst the lively and somewhat rowdy musketeers. A second company to guard the queen was mooted, but the expense of any musketeer seemed excessive to many courtiers at a time of war. Thus the Queen's Musketeers were not raised and, while on campaign, the Spanish King's Musketeers were disbanded on 23 June 1704, its men being incorporated into the Third Company of the Guardias de Corps (Life Guards).

In 1764, Empress Catherine II of Russia created the Corps of Chevaliers Gardes, the Knight's Guard, which became the more senior of the imperial bodyguard units. It was charged with the personal protection of the sovereign and thus was the most prestigious unit in the Russian army. During its existence, its members wore a *soubreveste* the same as the French King's Musketeers, but of scarlet instead of blue.

Troopers of the Brandenburg Trabaten-Garde, 1690. The elector of Brandenburg may have been fighting Louis XIV's Musketeers, but their repute was such that his guard unit was modelled after them. The Brandenburg guard troopers had a blue cassock with the elector's cross on it. Print after R. Knötel. Anne S. K. Brown Military Collection, Brown University Library, Providence, USA. (Author's photo)

Mosquetero de la Guardia, 1702–04. The Spanish version of France's King's Musketeers. They wore the same uniform as France's 1st Musketeer Company. Print after Giminez. Anne S. K. Brown Military Collection, Brown University Library, Providence, USA. (Author's photo)

THE LAST KING'S MUSKETEER

The widespread fame of the King's Musketeers lingered after the 1775 disbandment of the two companies. The heroic fights in battle, the jolly brawls, the duels, the good education, the secret missions and perhaps even the ghost of d'Artagnan – legendary in his own times – continued to lurk in the minds of many; there was something special and indefinable about being a King's Musketeer. The myth grew as years passed. After Napoleon's first abdication, the portly Louis XVIII assumed power and, on 15 June 1814, recreated the two companies of the King's Musketeer in his royal guard. While there were young men in the new companies, some 50 former musketeers that had been disbanded in 1775, now aged between 55 and 79, were also integrated into the new units, either for actual service or with honorary ranks if they were not equal to active duty. The other recruits were staunchly loyal royalists. Magnificent new uniforms were designed and made for these new musketeers (see below). Thus, their first appearance in public on 21 January 1815 made a sensation in fashionable Paris because of their beautiful uniforms and, in particular, their elaborate helmets. But public parades soon gave way to more serious events; Napoleon escaped his exile

King's Musketeers of the 1st (left) and 2nd (right) companies, 1814–15. Print after R. Knötel. Anne S.K. Brown Military Collection, Brown University Library, Providence, USA. (Author's photo)

on Elba and marched into Paris ousting the unpopular royal regime. On 27 March, part of the King's Musketeers dissolved while 57 musketeers (including eight officers) escorted the king to safety in Ghent. Following Napoleon's defeat at Waterloo in June, the royal government was restored in France and the King's Musketeers were re-formed. However, the high cost of the two companies as well as the actual usefulness of having such units as part of the guard came under scrutiny. The military school was certainly not what it had once been and the advanced age of many of its members made vigorous service difficult. The projected disbandment, scheduled to take place on 31 August 1815, obviously caused considerable repercussions in the corridors of power, resulting in a decree that extended the life of the units. On 31 December 1815, the abolitionists won and King Louis XVIII signed the order, immediately disbanding the King's Musketeers.

That might have been the last of the King's Musketeers as a unit, but their fame continued in literature in Alexandre Dumas's novels and in the arts, first on the stage and, from the early 20th century, the silver screen. This created worldwide fame for the King's Musketeers. To emulate a musketeer has since become a young lad's favourite pastime the world over. And why not? The real article two-and-a-half centuries ago was indeed a dashing fellow.

A young King's Musketeer of the 1st Company, 1814–15. Portrait by Henry d'Orfeuille. Musée de l'Armée, Paris. (Author's photo)

D'Artagnan of the King's Musketeers. The legendary likeness perpetuated in countless books and movies, and probably quite similar to the young swashbuckling d'Artagnan and his comrades. Statue by Gustave Doré sitting on the base of the monument to Alexandre Dumas unveiled in 1883 at the Place Général Catroux in Paris. (Wikimedia)

COLLECTING, MUSEUMS AND RE-ENACTMENT

Musketeer memorabilia is quite scarce and most of the known items on public display are in the Musée de l'Armée situated within the Invalides in Paris and the museum at Salon-de-Provence. Items from the 1622–46 King's Musketeers seem to have totally vanished. There are very few from the period of Louis XIV's reign and they consist mainly of pictorial works. The most impressive of these are the large, recently restored frescos in the halls of the Invalides, now occupied by museum exhibits. Fortunately, there are many more objects from the reign of Louis XV (1715–74), as can be seen in this book. Finally, many more items have survived the short-lived 1814–15 units who certainly had attractive uniforms and weapons. Those items accessible to private collectors are usually from the later Louis XV period and the 1814–15 formations; they are still very scarce and are usually exquisite and very attractive artefacts that command high prices. As for accurately and well-appointed King's Musketeer re-enactment units, they require substantial funds from individuals as well as facilities for maintaining the right type of horses, not to mention the intricate and highly decorated saddles and housings. With the correct uniform and weapons, this can easily amount to many, many thousands of pounds. Which is surely why one does not see many properly appointed King's Musketeer re-enactors.

SELECT BIBLIOGRAPHY

Bernard, Charles, *Histoire du roy Louis XIII*, Paris (1646)

Barrey, Pierre Edmond, *Précis historique sur la maison du roi, depuis sa formation en 1814, jusqu'à sa réforme en 1815*, Paris (1816)

Bordaz, Odile, *D'Artagnan, mousquetaire du roi*, Balzac-Le Griot, Paris (1990). The best documented recent study on d'Artagnan.

Bosson, Clément, 'Les Mousquetaires du roi et leurs armes' in *Gazette des armes*, No. 42 (October 1976)

Boullier, P.-J.-B., *Histoire des divers corps de la maison militaire des rois de France…*, Paris (1818)

Bourrassin, Émmanuel, 'Les gardes des reines-régentes, des princes du sang et des grands officiers de la couronne' in *Uniformes*, No. 119 (October 1988)

Chauviré, Frédéric, 'La Maison du Roi sous Louis XIV, une troupe d'élite' in *Revue historique des armées*, No. 242 (2006), pp. 114–21

Christian-Gérard & Lelièpvre, Eugène, *Maison bleue – maison rouge, cavaliers du roi soleil*, Paris (1945)

Churchill, Winston S., *Marlborough: His Life and Times*, Vol. 1, London (1933)

Daniel, Père Gabriel, *Histoire de la milice française…*, Vol. 2, Paris (1721)

Dumas, Alexandre, *Grand dictionnaire de la cuisine*, Paris (1878)

Du Verdier, Sieur, *Le vray et nouveau estat de la France comme elle est gouvernée en cette présente année 1656*, Paris (1656)

Gazette de France, Paris (1622, 1629 and 1633 editions)

Lacaze, Pierre, *En garde – Du duel à l'escrime*, Gallimard, Paris (1991)

L'État de la France, Paris (1642, 1661, 1672, 1677, 1678, 1684, 1687, 1692 and 1694 editions)

La Tour, Sieur de, *Précis historique des différentes gardes des rois François*, Paris (1764)

Le Thueux, M., *Essais historiques sur les deux compagnies des mousquetaires du roi de France, supprimées le 1er janvier 1776…*, 2 Vols, The Hague (1778)

Mac Carthy, M. Dugué, *La cavalerie française et son harnarche*ment, Maloine, Paris (1985)

Mac Carthy, M. Dugué, *La cavalerie au temps des chevaux*, Éditions Presse Audiovisuel, Paris (1989)

Michaud, Joseph François & Poujoulat, Jean Joseph François (eds), *Nouvelle collection des mémoires pour servir à l'histoire de France…*, Memoirs of Cardinal Richelieu (1837) Memoirs of Mademoiselle de Montpensier [nicknamed La Grande Demoiselle] & Memoirs of Montglay (1838), Paris

Mont, du & Rousset, *Le cérémonial diplomatique des cours de l'Europe…*, Vol. 1, Amsterdam (1739)

Noirmont, Dunoyer de & Marbot, Alfred de, *Costumes militaires français*, Paris (1846)

Pétard, Michel, *Des sabres et des épées: troupes à cheval de Louis XIV à l'Empire*, Vol. 1, Éditions du Canonnier, Nantes (1999)

Pétard, Michel, 'Les Mousquetaires du roi avant Fontenoy' in *Tradition*, No. 53 (June 1991)

Plaideux, Nicolas, 'Les mousquetaires de la garde du roi' in *Les grandes batailles de l'histoire*, No. 27 (July 1994)

Puysegur, Jacques de Chastenet de, *Mémoires…*, Vol. 1, Paris (1747)

Rouvroy, Louis, Duke of Saint-Simon, *Mémoires de Saint-Simon*, Vol. 1 (1879 edition)

Smith, George, *An Universal Military Dictionary*, London (1779)

Suzane, Louis, *Histoire de la cavalerie Française*, Vol. 1, Paris (1874)

Thion, Stéphane, *Les armées françaises de la guerre de Trente Ans*, LRT Éditions, Auzielle (2008)

GLOSSARY

Brigadier:
in the French army, the field officer's rank is brigadier-general; at the company level, a *brigadier* in the line cavalry is a senior NCO, but in the guard cavalry, he ranks as a junior captain. A *sous-brigadier* is a lower-rank NCO in the line cavalry, but in the guard cavalry ranks is a subaltern officer.

Cadet:
in military terms, a young gentleman training to become an officer; in general terms, a younger brother.

Cassock:
in French a *casaque*. Popular livery garment often worn by guard units, especially in the first half of the 17th century. Cassocks were usually in the colours of the livery of their master and bore an insignia on the breast and on the back. Replaced by the *soubreveste* (qv) from 1688.

Company:
in the King's Musketeers and other guards cavalry units could reach the strength of a line cavalry regiment. In the line cavalry, a company would have about 40 men.

Cornette:
cornet. The most junior officer rank in the line cavalry, also carries the standard, but ranks higher in the guards cavalry.

Enfants perdus:
the forlorn hope. 'Signifies men detached for several regiments or otherwise appointed to make the first attack… They are so called from the great danger they are unavoidably exposed to.' (G. Smith, 1779)

Escadron: squadron.
There were no squadrons in the King's Musketeers (not to be confused with *escouade*: squad). Squadrons in the line cavalry consisted of three or four companies.

Escouade: squad.
In the King's Musketeers, each company was divided into six squads that had about the same strength as a company in the line cavalry and each squad had its proportion of officers and a standard (not to be confused with *escadron*: squadron). In the line cavalry, a company had three to four squads of about ten troopers each.

Gendarmerie de France:
16 cavalry companies that were adjuncts to the guard and not part of the line cavalry. They were generally on campaign with the *maison du Roi* (qv). This corps was an elite cavalry division and bears no relation to the modern French police called the Gendarmerie.

Hand:
measure for ascertaining a horse's height. A hand measured four inches or 10.8mm. Thus, measured just in front of the saddle, a horse 15 hands high was 1.62m.

Maison du Roi:
or the King's household, more properly the *maison militaire du Roi*, which encompassed the guard units. The mounted ones were: the Gardes du Corps (four companies), the Gendarmes (one company), the Chevau-légers (one company), the Mousquetaires (two companies) and the Grenadiers à cheval (one company). See also: Gendarmerie de France.

Lettre de cachet:
a secret order from the king to arrest and detain a person discreetly, usually a high-ranking official.

NCO:	non-commissioned officer.
Maréchal de camp:	the French army's name for a major general, occasionally mistakenly translated as a marshal.
Maréchal des armées du roi:	the highest rank in the French army, equivalent to marshal in other armies.
Maréchal des logis:	at regimental level, the field officer specially tasked with lodging arrangements; at company level, a quartermaster sergeant. Has officer status in the King's Musketeers.
Mestre de camp:	equivalent to colonel of a regiment.
Musketeer:	in French a *mousquetaire* meaning an infantry soldier armed with a matchlock musket (a *mousquet*). From the late 17th and early 18th centuries, the flintlock musket (a *fusil*) was adopted and infantrymen became *fusiliers*. However, the King's Musketeers kept their old name of *mousquetaire*.
Schabraque or *shabraque*:	the cloth (or occasionally leather) blanket going under the saddle, equivalent to the English housings, and sometimes highly decorated with lace and embroidery.
Soubreveste:	a sleeveless jacket worn over the coat, richly trimmed and bearing an insignia on the breast and on the back.
Trooper:	an enlisted cavalryman; in French: *maître*.
Sous-brigadier:	see *Brigadier*.

The cat's trial in the Paris Parliament, 1720. A young musketeers' pranks knew no bounds and a peak of sorts was reached during a financial crisis of 10 July 1720. That day, the government had the King's Musketeer oust the legislators who were stubbornly opposed to its fiscal measures and occupy the Paris Parliament. Once that was done, the musketeers sat in the Great Chamber and held their own special session of Parliament: they blamed the nation's woes on a stray cat! After many grand debates, the cat was found guilty. Print after A. Robida. Private collection. (Author's photo)

INDEX